DUXHURST SURREY'S LOST VILLAGE

Ros Black

DUXHURST – SURREY'S LOST VILLAGE
Copyright © Ros Black 2011

Published by Arbe Publications, Reigate, Surrey RH2 0DY

ISBN 978-0-9569270-0-2

Book design by Agent Design
www.agentdesign.eu

Printed and bound in Great Britain by
CPI Antony Rowe, Chippenham and Eastbourne

*THIS BOOK IS DEDICATED
TO VIOLET ANTHONY*

Contents

Acknowledgements

I became fascinated by Duxhurst when I was researching *A Talent for Humanity*, my biography of the village's founder, Lady Henry Somerset. It soon became clear that the story of Duxhurst did not finish with Lady Henry's death.

Compiling the history of the village has been like putting together a jigsaw, without knowing the full picture, or how many pieces there were, or where they might be found. It has been my pleasure and privilege to meet some lovely people who have been happy to share with me their stories and knowledge.

New snippets of information are still surfacing. I very much hope that, after reading this book, more people will come forward with their stories of Duxhurst.

I am especially grateful to past and present residents of Duxhurst and their families: **Violet Anthony** and her son **John, Gina and Peter Knox, Peter Green, Kathy and Paul Early, Helena Herring, Neville Brown, William Constable, Pauline Hardy** and her mother **June, Caroline Howard, Maureen Cole, Graham Geal, Dave Gregory, Tony and Barry Morgan and Gordon Aspey.**

Diana Rose, Jane Bushell and **Brian Brown** shared with me the story of their mothers, Winnie and Ethel. **Doug Dew** contacted me with information about his grandmother, Lillian.

It was local historian, **Audrey Ward**, who first introduced me to the story of Lady Henry Somerset and I am deeply indebted to her for her unfailing support and enthusiasm for my researches. **Eileen Wood**, curator of **Reigate Priory Museum**, has also been most helpful as have **Mary Slade** and **Carol Sandford** of the **Holmesdale Natural History Museum**. I am indebted to other local historians, **Alan Moore, Sean Hawkins, Richard Cooper** and **Brian Buss** who have generously made photographs, postcards and archive material available to me. Thanks also must go to staff at **Surrey's History Centre** at Woking and to **Mark**

iii

Davison of the Surrey Mirror, who featured my research into Duxhurst in his Yesteryear column.

John Billingham, a trustee of The Royal Alexandra and Albert School, kindly provided me with a wealth of information about the days when The Alexandra Orphanage owned Duxhurst village.

Arthur Hutchinson's pictorial map of Duxhurst and **John Norsworthy's** account of the village, both produced in the 1980s, have been rich sources of inspiration and information.

James Hervey-Bathurst, owner of Eastnor Castle and grandson of Lady Henry Somerset's cousin, Arthur, kindly granted me access to the family archives, from which I learnt a great deal about Duxhurst's founder and the rationale behind the Duxhurst project. Eastnor Castle archivist Hazel Lein was especially helpful, as was her predecessor, Douglas Sylvanus-Davis. I also had the pleasure of meeting Lady Henry's great grandson, The Duke of Beaufort, and his wife at Badminton House.

I was able to access the archives of the National British Women's Temperance Association at Solihull, where the staff, led by **Mary Ayres** and **Mrs Stretton**, were very accommodating.

Duxhurst is not just a local story. In its early years, the village received many visitors from overseas, some being colleagues of Lady Henry Somerset in the temperance movement. Through my researches, new international friendships are being forged today. It was a great pleasure to meet **Janet Olson**, volunteer archivist at The Frances Willard Historical Association in Illinois, when she came to England recently, and to show her Duxhurst and Reigate Priory. I have corresponded with **Carolyn De Swarte Gifford**, an expert on Frances Willard, and **Olwen Claire Neissen**, a Canadian academic who wrote *Aristocracy, Temperance and Social Reform – the life of Lady Henry Somerset*.

Nearer to home, **Emmanuel Church, Sidlow**, is celebrating its own 150th anniversary in 2011 and is raising awareness of the Duxhurst heritage to local residents. Special thanks to the Rector, the **Rev. Bill Campen** and churchwardens **Liz Neale** and **Alf Turner** for granting me access to the Service Registers and Duxhurst items retained at their church. Other members of the congregation, **Tim Spinney, Michael Knight, Geoff and Audrey MacKrell, John and Edna Molyneux** have been helpful, enthusiastic and encouraging.

Extracts from the *News of the World* article in November 1965 are used under licence from *News International*. *Ideal Home Magazine* has kindly allowed me to reproduce several photographs of The Cottage at Duxhurst from their 1923 December issue.

All endeavours have been made to clear copyrights with owners of photographs used in this book. If, inadvertently, I have not acknowledged assistance or copyright, I offer my apologies and will be happy to rectify this in future editions.

Last, but not least, I wish to thank my friend **Rosemary Callinan**, who has been my 'critical eye' and my family – **Steve, Julia, Helen, Tom and Eduart** – for all their support.

THE PROLOGUE

*"We have seen women alter in the
sunshine of the atmosphere"*

Lady Henry Somerset 1896

A HIDDEN HERITAGE

The story of Duxhurst village is an intriguing one. It was a village conceived by the determination of one woman, Lady Henry Somerset, in the late nineteenth century. Yet, by the 1970s, it had all but disappeared. How and why it felt into disrepair is, even now, shrouded in a degree of mystery. Tales of black masses in the village church and raves in the manor house still surface occasionally.

As you journey south from Reigate along the A217 towards Gatwick airport, you can easily miss the entrance to Duxhurst Lane on the right hand side. It is a narrow, unsurfaced road, so not encouraging casual visitors. It is hard to imagine that on the 6th July 1896 that entrance had been decorated with a special arch proclaiming "Welcome to our Friends" to greet Mary, Duchess of Teck. The Duchess and a retinue of aristocratic ladies were there as guests of Lady Henry Somerset for the official opening of Duxhurst, as a "farm colony for inebriate women".

The Duchess was but one of many famous faces to grace the Duxhurst stage. More lowly characters also played their parts, shaped by the times and the very atmosphere of the place.

When the director – Lady Henry Somerset – died, other, less charismatic figures, struggled to continue the venture. But its time had been and gone. Like scenery discarded at the end of a performance, many of the Duxhurst buildings fell into ruin over the following decades. A few were rescued and renovated; many have been lost forever.

But when we forget a place, it is too easy to forget also the people who lived there and their stories of overcoming adversity and blossoming as human beings. As we will see, Duxhurst had a very special atmosphere and this did live on after Lady Henry's death. Those who lived on the estate in the 1940s, '50s and '60s still talk of it with great fondness. Today's residents of Duxhurst Lane feel privileged to enjoy their rural homes.

So let us explore the past, lift the lid off our hidden heritage and reveal the drama that was Duxhurst.

Somerset Cottage, formerly known as St Crispins, being renovated by Mr and Mrs Knox 1960. Photograph courtesy of Peter & Gina Knox.

A fascinating story is buried beneath the brambles and scrub wood we see today.

Lady Henry Somerset. Photograph courtesy of Holmesdale Natural History Museum.

ACT 1

"I wondered if there was in all this great and powerful England a spot of ground dearer to God than that on which the Farm Home Colony has raised its sacred walls"

Frances Willard,
American Temperance Leader

PRODUCER, DIRECTOR, STAR

To understand and appreciate the concept and successes of Duxhurst, we must first understand the personality and motivations of its founder.

In her day, Lady Henry Somerset was compared to Florence Nightingale. She topped a poll of readers of the London Evening News as the person they would most like as the first female Prime Minister. Yet today she is not well known, perhaps because she championed the temperance cause and this has long gone out of fashion.

The story of her life is fascinating; the list of her achievements long and varied. She overcame the sorrow of an unhappy marriage to become a leading social reformer, a powerful orator who could pack halls around Britain and throughout America. She promoted women's issues well before feminism became a popular movement.

Isabel Caroline Somers Cocks was the eldest daughter of Charles, 3rd Earl Somers. Her mother, Virginia, was a renowned socialite and beauty. The family owned great swathes of land in Herefordshire and Worcestershire, including Eastnor Castle near Ledbury, as well as most of the town of Reigate in Surrey where they had a fine country house, Reigate Priory. They also owned much of the less salubrious Somers Town, in the St Pancras area of London.

In 1872, as a shy twenty year-old, Isabel married Lord Henry Somerset, second son of the Duke of Beaufort. A glittering life of aristocratic pleasures seemed to lie ahead of her. Sadly, her hopes of a happy marriage and a large family were dashed within days of her society wedding; the honeymoon at Reigate Priory was a disaster.

To Isabel's dismay, her husband announced he wanted them to lead separate lives. She could not understand what she had done wrong. For a brief period marital relations were resumed and a son was born. But Isabel could not turn a blind eye to her husband's behaviour. For Lord Henry was a homosexual and at that time, homosexuality was not just frowned upon, it was a crime.

It took Lady Henry several difficult years to escape from the marriage. In challenging her husband, Comptroller of the Queen's Household and a protégé of Disraeli, for custody of their son, she flouted all the social conventions of the period. She may have won the court case, but it was a hollow victory as she was the one then shunned by society. Gossip spread that she had "invented a new sin", something only mentioned in the Bible and gentlemen did not want their wives associating with her.

For several years, Lady Henry nursed her hurt pride, living primarily at Reigate Priory. It was here that she had a moment of divine revelation. As she sat under the shade of a tree by the Priory lake, weighed down by worries, she queried the very existence of God. Then, as she later recounted, she heard a voice as if from deep within herself saying, "Act as if I am and thou shalt know I am." From that time on, her religious conviction never waivered. Although, at one stage, she flirted with Methodist teaching, in later life she became increasingly High Anglican.

Following the death of her father, she moved back to Eastnor where she began to visit the sick and needy. Distressed by the alcohol-fuelled squalor of Ledbury's Bye Street, she set up a mission and encouraged people to sign the Total Abstinence Pledge. She led by example and took the pledge herself.

In 1890, Lady Henry became President of the British Women's Temperance Association (BWTA) and set about expanding its remit, refusing to be the titled figurehead some people had thought they were electing.

When not on the campaign trail, arguing for the restriction of opening hours rather than the full prohibition favoured by her American colleagues, she preferred to offer practical help. She set up homes in both Eastnor and Reigate where young girls, often from the workhouse, could be trained for domestic service. She established a settlement in the East End of London.

Lady Henry was one of those women who always had to be busy. She was multi-talented: an author, journalist, artist and sculptor. Most importantly, she had what Chekhov described as "a talent for humanity". Despite her own health problems, she espoused many social causes, not just those relating to drug and alcohol abuse.

Lady Henry Somerset (right) with her friend Frances Willard.

Her friendship with the American temperance leader, Frances Willard, brought her some comfort but she was at times extremely lonely. She chastised herself for being interested in the theatre and the arts and even society gossip and always thought she could be doing more for others less fortunate than herself.

She was a woman who saw not only the bigger picture – a liquor trade which was almost uncontrolled, due to vested interests and the ability of governments around the world to raise taxes from its sale – but also the intimate portrait of the family or individual whose life had been blighted by alcohol abuse.

She would campaign tirelessly, lobbying governments and politicians of all parties. She would address huge rallies, leading carriage processions round Hyde Park. She would go down the pits to talk to miners about God's love for them.

She even bought her own newspaper, the *Woman's Herald*, which later evolved into *Woman's Signal*, to promulgate her message of restraint.

But words, however powerful and eloquently delivered, were not enough for Lady Henry Somerset. Action was required; action which made a real difference to the lives of real people, whatever their class or rank in society; action which proved without words that each person was valued, whatever their circumstances.

Her own experience as a victim of society's harsh and ill-informed censure, following her separation from her husband, gave her a special empathy with those less fortunate. "Only those who can change places, and find themselves in the position of the sufferer or sinner, have the power to help or comfort them," she wrote. Her marital breakdown also gave her the sense to realize that there was often a story behind a person's behaviour which was not always apparent to the casual observer. It meant

The campaigner, frequently interviewed in the press.

The passionate carer.

she started to look into the causes of alcoholism, not just the effects.

Lady Henry's cousin and staunch supporter, the Reverend E. F. Russell, recounted another reason for her compassion for women suffering from alcohol and drug abuse. "… her own dearest friend, a lady of great gifts, and great charm, fell a victim to the seductive habit [excessive alcohol consumption], which dragged her gradually down, until at last she perished by her own hand."

Lady Henry was very strong-willed and not afraid to fight for her beliefs. Not surprisingly, her approach upset some of her fellow campaigners and under her presidency there were many internal battles within the British Women's Temperance Association. In 1893 the inevitable happened and those who did not agree with her reforming agenda broke away to form their own Women's Total Abstinence Union.

This gave Lady Henry more scope to progress some of her schemes. Whilst the BWTA had had a house at Sydenham for the care of inebriate women, Isabel was content for this to go to the breakaway faction. She had grander ideas. She didn't just want a house, she wanted a whole village.

In November 1893, she secured the passing of a resolution of the

9

Annual Council of the renamed National British Women's Temperance Association (NBWTA) to launch an appeal for funds to establish an Industrial Farm Village. And just three miles south of her own Reigate home, she found the perfect site - Duxhurst.

A fuller account of the life of this amazing woman can be found in my book *A Talent for Humanity – The life and work of Lady Henry Somerset* published in 2010. ISBN 978-1-9052-0093-1

THE SHOW BEGINS

The purchase of the Duxhurst estate, initially on a long lease, was not without its problems and it didn't help that at this stage Lady Henry was spending a considerable amount of time in America, where she proved a popular speaker. The Americans were dazzled by her English aristocratic charm and persuaded by her knowledge and enthusiasm for the temperance cause. She had to make a short visit back to England specifically to ensure the land deal went ahead on acceptable terms.

In the fourteenth century the Duxhurst area had been owned by Chertsey Abbey. The abbot, John de Rutherwyck, granted it to Peter de Duxhurst to be held "of the Abbey". By the time it was sold to Christ's Hospital in 1602, Duxhurst was considered a manor. The hospital used a legacy from Dame Mary Ramsey, widow of the Lord Mayor of London, to purchase various parcels of land in Surrey as an investment. Almost three centuries later, it was only Lady Henry's personal plea to the Duke of York, one of the trustees, which persuaded the hospital to sell the estate.

The NBWTA carefully avoided taking on full responsibility for the project, either managerially or financially. Yet they made some significant contributions. In their 1894 Annual Report the Association recorded the fact that £2000 had already been collected for the new village, including a generous gift of £500 from Miss Sarah Hinton of Cheltenham.

As a site for the project, Duxhurst was ideal. With views of the North Downs, nestled in woodland and fields, it met the obvious requirement of being several miles from the nearest public house.

There was an added bonus – it already had a Manor House which could be made fit and ready for occupation without spending lots of time and money on it. Such a manor house was very appropriate for ladies of high social status, for there was a recognition that alcohol abuse was not solely the province of the working classes.

Some patients could be admitted here whilst other parts of the village were being built. A separate house, Hope Cottage, on the fringes of the

Duxhurst estate was also acquired. This may be the Hope Cottage which still exists on Ironsbottom today. Hope Cottage was intended for middle class women who could afford to pay a little towards their costs.

The working class women would be housed in brand new accommodation in the centre of the village, in charming cottages around a village green.

Although Lady Henry Somerset deserves the main credit for establishing Duxhurst, there were other members of the temperance movement who contributed ideas and considerable effort.

Indeed, it was a Dr Sarah Anderson Brown whom Lady Henry herself credits with proposing the original idea for a farm colony. She had studied methods used in different parts of the world, including Germany and America. The work of Sherburne prison in Massachusetts, where prisoners were put to work looking after live animals, supported Dr Brown's view that direct contact with nature was beneficial. Lady Henry took no convincing.

Her views were reinforced by an account she read of the work done by Pastor von Bodelschwing amongst those suffering from epilepsy. "As I read of these village homes I realized that just such a treatment might be applied to other cases of diseased humanity, and that alcoholism could be treated in just the same way," Lady Henry later explained.

Lady Henry used all her contacts and had detailed plans drawn up for the village. She knew she would have to start with just a few cottages, but allow room for more to be built as funds were raised.

The first patients were actually admitted in late 1894, with some others joining the little community in 1895. Yet Lady Henry's regular absences abroad meant that the NBWTA felt it unwise to open the home formally that year.

Responsibility for the project was provisionally given to a small committee and they reported that they had received "great encouragement in their work." The sub-committee clearly felt very wary of their new role. They soon resolved to appoint Lady Henry as 'Superintendent' of the Association's grandly-styled 'Department of the Industrial Farm Home for Inebriate Women' and agreed that the whole organization and management of Duxhurst should be left in her hands. The National

Executive of the Association did however fund one of the cottages which was named 'Isabel' in honour of their president.

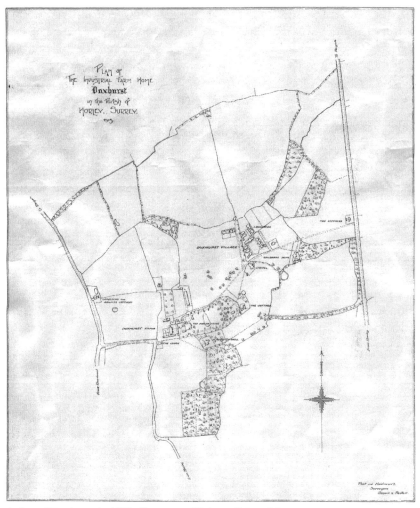

A plan of Duxhurst in 1913. Courtesy of Reigate Priory Museum.

Such were the demands on her time that even Lady Henry had to concede that she couldn't be everywhere, so she appointed a matron, Eleanor Camell, to supervise the project. This did not mean, however, that she had lost interest in the village even before it had become fully operational. She was a mother whose son was about to attain his majority; she was busy extending and altering Reigate Priory and she had a hectic schedule of speaking engagements on both sides of the Atlantic. Her new found American friends, particularly Frances Willard, took up a lot of her time. There were also articles to be written, sketches to be made, bicycles to be ridden.

The Duxhurst village actually became the centre of Lady Henry's later life. For she saw, in its work, the proof of her belief that inebriate women could be cured; that through kindness and compassion they could be steered towards a better life and develop the inner strength to ensure that when they left the village they did not return to their old ways. "In every case of drunkenness, or drug-addiction, that mysterious mechanism called the Will has been put out of working order, and until it has been restored to its proper balance, nothing of permanent value has been done".

By the time of the official opening on 6th July 1896, Duxhurst was a thriving community. All the fund raising and impassioned speeches had paid off and six cottages had been built and occupied around the manicured green, with two others already under construction.

ROYAL COMMAND PERFORMANCE

Following the scandal of her marriage breakdown, Isabel was not received formally at Court for several years, although her mother, Lady Somers, had remained on friendly terms with the Royal Family. By the 1890s, however, Lady Henry was once again in favour and she was able to persuade Mary, Duchess of Teck, to carry out the formal opening of Duxhurst.

The Duchess travelled from her home at White Lodge in Richmond Park to Reigate Priory, where she was entertained to lunch by Lady Henry. Other guests included the Duchess of St Albans (her son's mother-in-law), her sister Adeline, Duchess of Bedford, the Duchess of Marlborough, Lord William Bereford, Sir William and Lady Lawson, the Dean of Hereford, Sir Algernon West and the Hon. Henry Cubitt, MP. Also present was Lady Henry's great friend, the American temperance leader, Frances Willard. From Frances's wry account of the day, we learn that wine was served at lunch but that many people abstained and that the untitled guests, such as herself, were very much in the minority.

Postcard courtesy of Alan Moore.

An impressive carriage procession then headed the three miles south to Duxhurst, cheered on by local crowds. As the Royal party entered the village, the Redhill band struck up the national anthem.

The Duchess of Teck was given a short tour of the cottages before she laid the foundation stones of two new ones. Then Lady Henry read a welcoming address on behalf of the hundred thousand women of the NBWTA. On the village green "purses" or donations were officially handed over, totalling almost three hundred pounds, followed by a presentation from the Kent Temperance Association specifically for the hospital building. The fund-raising didn't stop there though. Goods made in the Duxhurst workshops were on sale in the recreation hall, as were postcards of the village.

Whilst the majority of the visitors enjoyed tea in a marquee, the Duchess and other high-ranking guests had their refreshments on the secluded lawn of the Manor House. The Duchess stayed later than expected and seemed suitably impressed by all she saw. Following the official opening, the Duchess continued to support Lady Henry's work, often from her private purse.

THE VILLAGE

L ady Henry used a local Reigate firm, W. Bagaley & Sons, for the building of the cottages. They were fairly basic in construction, of lathe and plaster, but charming in appearance, with tall chimneys and their tin roofs covered in thatch; a far cry from the crammed, squalid conditions to which most of the patients were accustomed.

Not every cottage was identical but they each had the same basic features: a sitting room or parlour, a kitchen and pantry, a bedroom for the matron or House Sister and smaller bedrooms for six to twelve patients, with a coalhouse and W.C. tacked on the side. Each was decorated and furnished in a simple, but homely, style, "gay with pictures and flowers and bright-coloured chintz."

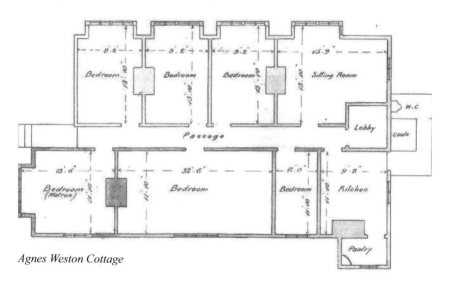

Agnes Weston Cottage

Initially the cottages were named after benefactors – hence Derby, Liverpool and Birmingham, funded by the respective local temperance branches. Another was named 'Massingbred' as it was paid for by Mrs Massingbred, a wealthy temperance supporter, to mark her son's birthday.

Miss Weston was a tireless temperance crusader amongst the sailors and much respected for her efforts.

This generous lady made many subsequent donations to Duxhurst.

There was also the 'Agnes Weston' cottage, funded by the Plymouth branch and officers and men of the Royal Navy.

At the head of the village green was a large hall, paid for by Lady Henry herself. This hall was initially called the 'Margaret Bright Lucas' building, after Lady Henry's predecessor as president of the BWTA. With offices, kitchens, bathrooms, dining room and recreation room (known as the 'Willard Hall' in honour of the American temperance leader), it was the hub of village activity. Meetings and concerts were held there and every day the patients would come together for their main meals, making friends from other cottages, hearing all the gossip and becoming, as Lady Henry put it, "a citizen of this city in miniature."

There was a big emphasis on creating a sense of belonging to a community, both physically within the village and emotionally. "When she [a woman patient] thought herself an outcast from society, she has found herself a member of that richest and best of all social circles – Humanity itself," said Lady Henry.

We know a great deal about the philosophy behind Duxhurst because Lady Henry wrote a book *Beauty for Ashes* which was published in 1913. Its primary purpose was to raise funds for the village but it provides us with a unique insight into the workings of the project.

Duxhurst was intended to be very different from the usual institutions of the time. Lady Henry had seen enough of these to know what worked and what didn't. "Great bare rooms, whitewashed walls and chill cleanliness" were not Duxhurst's style. The place was to be 'homely', first and foremost, with no locks or walls to keep the residents in.

The reception of new patients was therefore key. Many were distraught at leaving their children and homes, "full of doubt for the future and shame for the past." So they were always greeted by a cheerful-looking nurse and shown around. Lady Henry paints the scene: "Generally a new patient arrives in the afternoon, brought by her husband or a friend, or a convicted case is brought to us from prison in charge of warders, or from the Courts by a Police Court Missionary. In the cheerful Hospital kitchen, tea has been prepared, everything is dainty and clean ... After tea, the husband or friend, is shown around the rest of the Hospital, sees the patient's corner of the bright little ward. Then they are taken round the Colony, across the Village green to the other cottages and the Children's Home, to the Church and the Garden." This must have been reassuring to both patient and family.

Every new patient was initially assessed in the village hospital, which was situated very close to the cottages. "In the majority of cases, amongst working women at least, the beginnings of drunkenness has been connected with some bodily ailment." How important, therefore, to ensure these physical needs were attended to as a priority. "The woman must find recognition and sympathy for the real ills of her body, and until these are set right, the ills of the mind, for her at least, do not exist."

The Hospital as pictured in Beauty for Ashes.

The hospital nurses would also be trained to anticipate and manage the withdrawal symptoms, "the moods of depression and restlessness" caused by the craving for alcohol.

Some of the women who were admitted to Duxhurst were addicted not to alcohol but to drugs, which were surprisingly easy to obtain in the late nineteenth century. Cocaine and opium were the most common. Lady Henry cited the example of a lady who had been able, on one single visit to a chemist, to purchase seventy two boxes of opium pills. No wonder she declared drugs were sold "with criminal carelessness." In the hospital women were weaned off such drugs, their daily dose being reduced gradually.

Following this stay in hospital, a new patient would be allocated to their new home, "a home without a capital 'H'" as Lady Henry described it.

The aristocratic ladies would join their peers in the Manor House and were encouraged, but not forced, to join in with village activities. Their accommodation was much grander than the new, simple cottages and they even held occasional, alcohol-free, dinner parties in the dining room, or took tea on the manicured lawns down by the pond.

Women at work in the Duxhurst gardens, pictured in Beauty for Ashes

It might seem surprising that the hierarchy of social class was replicated at Duxhurst but one must remember that this was still Victorian England. Upper class families would have been very unwilling for their wives and daughters to go to any place which did not recognize their status. What is actually more surprising is the way in which Duxhurst broke down the social barriers.

For these fine ladies usually found themselves drawn into village life, even when this meant mixing with working class women. As we shall see, there were three main attractions – the beautiful church, the children and the gardens.

Before a newly admitted working class woman left the hospital, she would be allocated to a cottage, where she would live with a group of women under the watchful eye of the House Sister. Many of the staff had been recruited from the Church Army, selected for their compassion and common sense. Lady Henry was wise enough to appreciate that just as each patient was an individual, so were the staff, and each had their strengths and weaknesses. She described how some of the Sisters would work better with the younger women, others with the middle-aged; some best with the Bohemian type, others with those more conventional. Care was also taken, wherever possible, to avoid clashing personalities within the same cottage, although one can imagine the atmosphere becoming quite lively at times, especially when a new face was introduced.

By the time *Beauty for Ashes* was published in 1913, Lady Henry was widely acknowledged as an expert in the field of care for inebriates but as she wrote: "When the idea of a Farm Colony for Inebriate Women was first mooted it met with little else than ridicule. In those days a woman drunkard, when she was not an object of mirth, was an object for the scorn and contempt of the virtuous … To attempt to reform her was a waste of time and energy and could only be the enterprise of sentimental philanthropy."

It must have given her a great deal of satisfaction to prove people wrong and she took care to provide statistics to demonstrate her claims of a 73% success rate amongst women who stayed for at least a year.

Yet far more fascinating and, one senses, far more important to Lady Henry, were the individual stories of women finding hope, contentment and salvation at Duxhurst.

THE WOMEN

The story of one young woman who came to Duxhurst shows how easy it was for anyone, whatever their social status, to succumb to alcohol abuse. Most of the case studies cited by Lady Henry in *Beauty for Ashes* were anonymous, so, for ease, we will refer to this lady as Elizabeth.

Elizabeth's husband was a businessman, owner of several licensed premises in a city in the north of England. Although his wife had not lived on any of the premises, she had still managed to acquire both a taste for, and supplies of, alcohol. The poor man was distraught, blaming himself for her downfall and declaring her to be "the best woman in all the world before this habit laid hold of her." It was he who pleaded with Lady Henry to accept Elizabeth as a patient at Duxhurst.

Elizabeth seemed to want to be cured and showed "a pathetic desire to do well." She took to spending much of her time in the church, cleaning and tidying and making it ready for services "with an almost passionate love." Then, after just six months at Duxhurst, she was called back to help with her husband's business, which was in financial difficulties. Now the couple could not afford to maintain a home away from the licensed premises. Elizabeth had to live there and to serve in the bar, surrounded by temptation.

"Something had entered deeper into her soul than we knew," wrote Lady Henry. For she had been delighted to receive a letter from Elizabeth, which told how well she was coping. She had found a priest and taken instruction in preparation for confirmation and was trying hard to lead "a godly and sober life."

Elizabeth stayed in touch with staff and gave Duxhurst a simple, but glowing testimonial: "The Homes at Duxhurst have been my salvation. There I found everything that makes life worth living."

At the other end of the social spectrum we have the case of Molly, a tall Irishwoman, "an untamed amazon" who recounted with delight how she had once picked up a policeman like a puppy and carried him by the scruff of his neck across the street. Such exploits inevitably landed her in prison but one day she was sent instead to Duxhurst.

Initially, things did not go well. After a while she was sent back to prison but later returned to Duxhurst. Lady Henry's description of Molly tells us so much about how she was able to see behind the façade of someone's behaviour. "She could neither read nor write, but she had a heart, a heart that could love and respond to love. Smothered by the ashes of the wretched, wasted past, underneath all the rubbish, there was a burning ember which had never been extinguished, and this, we knew, could be fanned into flame by love."

In time, Molly responded to the trust the staff placed in her. The key, in Molly's case, was children. She was allowed to help with the care of some of the children in the village. "Her stern face would soften and then ripple in smiles when with unerring instinct a child sought her help."

Women and children share the laundry chores, Beauty for Ashes

I suspect this lady, whom Lady Henry herself identified as Molly, may be the same woman referred to by Lillian Brown, whose memories of her childhood at Duxhurst were recorded in the 1980s. Lillian described how there were two Irish women, Margaret and Molly who often used to argue, "which was very funny and laughable by anyone hearing them as they quarrelled in Irish." But when they had finished, "you could see them both cuddling each other and asking God to bless them. They were so loveable to all of us children."

One of the most detailed case histories Lady Henry recounts in her book is of a woman who was admitted to Duxhurst under The Inebriates Act of 1899. Two of the village cottages had been registered to receive such women, as an alternative to prison. Lady Henry does not give this woman's name but let us call her Mary.

Mary was a heavy drinker, "terror of the neighbourhood in which she lived." Several of her babies had died in infancy and there was a suspicion that she had been too drunk to care for them properly. Her husband had left her.

At Duxhurst, Mary resisted all attempts to engage with the religious ethos of the village. After two years, she was permitted to go out on licence, but she was brought back, drunk, by two policemen. At the end of her three year sentence, Mary was still difficult and known for her terrible temper. Lady Henry and her staff were unwilling to cast her adrift, as she had no home to return to, so they found her work on the colony. "She was allowed some liberty and a little money, in order to test her reliability," Lady Henry tells us.

For a few months, all seemed to be going well, until the day Mary came back late from her walk, well under the influence of drink. She apologized, was forgiven and returned to work. After a few more months of good behaviour, she was given a better position and seemed to respond. Then, one day, she quarrelled with a fellow worker and walked out, not to be seen again for over twenty four hours. "Late the following night, a weary, foot-sore figure, soaked with the beating rain, walked up our path. Silently she gave herself into our hands, crushed and broken. She was put to bed and left to rest. No word was said to her, no question asked, no reproach uttered."

It was only when Mary acknowledged her own problem and asked, "Why do I sink lower than a beast?" that staff felt the time was right to tell her that it was because she had turned her back on God's love and forgiveness. The suggestion was made that Mary return, not as a worker, but as a patient, to the colony, paying for her own keep with some of the money she had earned, "to face the others, and to show her penitence." She was warned it would not be easy. Bravely, Mary accepted the challenge and, no doubt to everyone's relief, became a changed person, going out of her way "to do little acts of kindness which amazed her former companions."

Eventually Mary asked if she could retract her denial of God and be prepared for confirmation. "We told her that the door of her heart opened from within, that her saviour had with infinite love and patience been waiting outside that door these many years."

Her husband took a lot of convincing that she was a changed person but eventually, reluctantly, he came to visit her at Duxhurst. He was so impressed that he agreed to take her back. A year later he wrote to staff at Duxhurst, to tell them of the wonderful change he had seen in his wife and how he now realized that this was God's work. He, too, was now preparing for his confirmation.

At the next Old Patients' Day, when former residents were invited to return to Duxhurst, Mary and her husband came long, bringing their young baby with them. We "thanked God that crooked things had been made straight," declared Lady Henry.

One of the most distinguished patients at Duxhurst was the Canadian opera singer, Georgina Sterling, whose stage name was Marie Toulinguet. Whilst on a hectic European tour, Georgina strained her vocal chords, so could not sing. Depression and alcohol dependence followed. Her sister, Janet, herself a nurse living in England, arranged for her to be admitted to Duxhurst in 1906 where she stayed for long periods over the next twenty years. Janet also moved to Duxhurst, to work as a nurse in the village. The country life-style seemed to suit Georgina. She earned the nickname 'Lady of the Lavender' as she was often to be found picking and drying bunches from the lavender fields.

THE NOTORIOUS JANE CAKEBREAD

Photograph from Beauty for Ashes

Looking at this rural scene, it would be easy to assume all the women were genteel, honest and hard-working but in many cases this was far from the reality, especially when they first arrived. For Lady Henry could often be found in the London courts pleading with magistrates to send habitual drunkards to Duxhurst rather than to jail, even when, in some instances, they had been in and out of prison many times.

One of Duxhurst's most famous cases, that of Jane Cakebread, did not turn out to be a major success. Lady Henry did not shy away from discussing the matter in her book, for she felt her methods, and the Duxhurst concept, had been unjustly attacked in some sectors of the press.

Jane Cakebread had been in prison some two hundred and eighty times before Lady Henry was asked to interview her at Holloway prison. Lady Henry described her as "in no ordinary sense an inebriate. She was an insane woman who became dangerously violent when drunk."

Jane revelled in her notoriety. Articles and academic papers were written about her. Her case was one of the primary reasons for the passing of the Habitual Inebriates Act of 1898, with the Lord Chancellor describing her numerous jail sentences as "a perfect scandal." Indeed the Act was often referred to as 'The Jane Cakebread Act'. Rudyard Kipling even christened his Lanchester car 'Jane Cakebread' because it gave him so much trouble.

It was often said that Jane enjoyed her court appearances so much that she left the magistrates smiling. But there was a darker side to her personality. She was described as "vain, jealous, untruthful and deficient in self-control." One of her doctors said "her inhibition was so affected [by alcohol] that she passed suddenly and almost instantaneously from blandness and graciousness to blasphemy, vituperation, and abuse."

Jane readily admitted to a weakness for "two penny drops of rum." She also had delusions of being a fine lady. At that first interview she regaled Lady Henry with tales of times past when she had driven in a trap to see the hunt and all the gentlemen in red coats had touched their hats to her. Thomas Holmes, the police-court missionary, as usual, was pleading Jane's case. He later explained that a £100 legacy had fed Jane's delusions of grandeur. The fact that the colony's owner was an aristocrat no doubt helped persuade Jane that Duxhurst was a suitable place for her, though she later complained of feeling "buried alive" in the country.

Lady Henry agreed to take Jane to Duxhurst but Jane managed just three months there - "three, perhaps, of the most difficult and unpleasant months of our work," recalled Lady Henry. When sober, Jane was difficult. When drunk she was violent. There were many instances of her throwing things around in the church and abusing staff and fellow residents.

Lady Henry's assessment, that Jane was insane and utterly irresponsible, was ignored by the authorities. Following several incidents, Lady Henry felt she had to let her leave Duxhurst. Inevitably, Jane was back in prison within days and there assaulted a prison officer. She was then committed to the Claybury lunatic asylum. Lady Henry did not mince her words. "Thus the point was proved that a woman had been kept in prison several hundred times who should have been committed to a lunatic asylum years before, and so saved money to the State and untold suffering and disgrace to the poor, wandering life."

What Lady Henry doesn't say in her book is that an article in the *Pall Mall Gazette* blamed her "mischievous interference" for Jane's insanity and committal. This slur could not be left unchallenged if Duxhurst was to succeed, so Lady Henry sued the editor, Lord Astor, for libel. The case was settled with Lord Astor issuing an apology and paying costs. Duxhurst's growing reputation was slightly battered but not irrevocably damaged.

So infamous had Jane Cakebread become that when she died, still an inmate of the asylum, news of her death was reported throughout the world. *The New York Times* used the lurid headline, "Death of the World's Awful Example".

The distinction between an 'habitual drunkard' and an 'insane person' was something Lady Henry stressed. She compared the case of Jane Cakebread with that of Annie Adams, another notorious frequenter of the London courts, nicknamed 'The Terror of Holloway'.

Having been charged for the hundred and sixth time with drunkenness, Annie agreed to stay in jail for a while until a place at Duxhurst became available for her. The police-court missionary, Thomas Holmes, was once again involved. He worked closely with Lady Henry on many cases and had great faith in her methods. He, too, seemed to recognize that Annie was quite different from Jane.

"Directly this person [Annie] was sober, she was pathetically tractable, and we recognized in her a true inebriate – a sane person who had been constantly overcome by the effects of alcohol, but whose mind regained its balance under normal conditions," wrote Lady Henry.

After a year at Duxhurst, no longer "a slave to her temptation", Annie left, determined to remain sober. Sadly, she died of pneumonia, just a short time later.

There were other occasions when Duxhurst hit the headlines for all the wrong reasons. In 1899, Bertha Peterson was charged with the murder of John Whibley, just days after she had been given notice from her position as a cottage sister at Duxhurst, because of her increasingly erratic mental state.

Inevitably there were some women who chose to abscond, but such instances were rare. Most responded over time to the non-judgmental approach of the village.

ST MARY AND THE ANGELS

No village would be complete without its church, certainly not a village designed by Lady Henry.

Initially the church was very simple and small, sited just across from the village green by the track to Lady Henry's own house, The Cottage.

This image is from a Christmas card which Lady Henry sent out in 1896 from Reigate Priory.

It was dedicated on 30th May 1986, with a special service led by Canon Wilberforce of Westminster, a supporter of the temperance movement. Lady Henry was keen to ensure the local clergy were also involved with the village, so the parish rector, the Reverend Aston Whitlock assisted. At this stage the village choir would not have been well-established, but the women were joined for this special occasion by girls from one of Lady Henry's other local enterprises, St Mary's Home in Reigate, and also by children of The Guild of Poor Things, a charity supported by her family.

Many members of the NBWTA were present, as the dedication of the Duxhurst church was also the first service of the Association's twentieth Annual Meeting. Frances Willard, visiting from America, described the day in her usual effusive style:

"And when it was all over, as I stood watching the long procession of brakes, filled by those noble women of the Executive Committee who are the special co-workers of their great leader [Lady Henry Somerset]; as I saw the little crippled fellows in their crimson blouses, shouting, 'Three cheers for Canon Wilberforce' ...; as I saw the women, who are the objects of so much loving thought, going quietly to their peaceful cottages, and the gentle Sisters in uniform, who have them in their care, I wondered if there was in all this great and powerful England a spot of ground dearer to God than that on which the Farm Home Colony has raised its sacred walls."

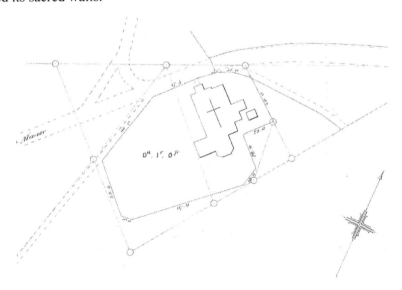

Extract from 1912 plan

Perhaps surprisingly, the church was not orientated towards the east as most churches are. It was entered through a gate directly from the main lane. Beside it was a small graveyard.

Lady Henry called it "The centre of our work, and the centre of our lives, the quiet spot holds for us memories which are part of the history of our souls."

The robed choir enters the extended church. Photo from Beauty for Ashes

Gradually the church became more ornate and had several extensions, including a new aisle in 1914. There were also various dedication services, including one for the chancel in 1901. Like most of the buildings in the village, the church had roses growing up its walls. It was designed to look welcoming, not austere.

The number and pattern of services changed over the years, becoming what we would now term High Church, yet Lady Henry was always keen to describe the village as non-denominational and inclusive of all faiths. She recognized that visitors were often surprised by all the religious statues and imagery around the village, but she declared that "ritual was a great help to faith." She erected a large crucifix from Ober Ammergau in the grounds near her cottage, which caused some controversy amongst her temperance association colleagues.

Some of the service records for the church have been preserved and are held at Emmanuel Church at Sidlow. Thus we know that in 1901, there were three services each Sunday - Holy Communion, Matins and Evensong. As the years went by, there were several confirmation services, often carried out by the Bishop of Kingston. Other high ranking bishops would come to Duxhurst; for example in February 1910, the Bishop of London visited.

From diary extracts quoted in *Lady Henry Somerset*, Kathleen Fitzpatrick's 1923 biography of Lady Henry, we can see that she was not always impressed by such visitors: "The Bishop came before Church. I was terribly disappointed because he only talked about the cat, nothing seemed to interest him. I did not care for his address – he was tired – for it seemed to me very lifeless ... I wonder if men like that ever understand what a word of encouragement means to us ..."

On two occasions, services had to be cancelled; once in January 1903 when icy roads meant the officiant arrived very late and once when there was a bicycle accident on the main road. There are also references to special services on the annual Old Patients' Day and to visiting missionaries.

A children's service was introduced in 1906. On Christmas Eve, the children would be taken from the church to a special crèche in the recreation room where they would have another short service, with short readings and carols. On the 26th December 1908, a Bethlehem Tableau was presented, the programme for which was written neatly in the back of the Service Register.

The church was always open, offering a place of quiet contemplation and calm. Women and children alike would find joy and comfort there.

"Drunkards and criminals cannot be reformed – let us be quite frank about it – but much more can be done for them, they can be redeemed ... we can do nothing for the body unless we first take account of the soul, and each is made to minister to the other ..."

THE CHILDREN

Throughout the whole drama of Duxhurst, children have played a major role. Initially the Nest was built as a holiday home, where children from the London slums could come down for a week or two, as respite from their harsh lives. Much of the money for the building was provided by Lady Henry's mother, Lady Somers.

Like most educated Victorians, Lady Henry believed in the benefits of country air. Indeed, her own mother had often removed her two daughters to the coast if she felt they were succumbing to a chill. But it wasn't just physical health which Lady Henry thought could be improved in the country. She knew it offered a magical world of escape, one which fuelled the imagination. She described this vividly in her own novel *Under the Arch of Life*, written in 1906. Billy, a young urchin, was asked if he would like to go to the country:

"He had heard so much about it from the boys who had been there. They had told him of the thousands of fields where everyone might play, and the woods full of bears and gypsies, and the wild horses that you might ride if you caught them, of the fish they had seen jumping out of the river, and the worms going about at night with lamps on their heads."

Within a couple of years, the Nest became a permanent home for children. Occasionally children were admitted along with their mothers, although they would live separately in the village. Usually, however, they came alone, referred by ministers, the NSPCC, the Salvation Army or the courts. They arrived, often traumatized, with fear in their eyes, having suffered cruelly at the hands of one or both of their parents. They had endured beatings and kickings and had often been starved; "their little bodies were covered in dirt and sores; they had big black bruises on their limbs ...

"They once were somebody's children, but they are trying to forget it, so don't mention 'mother' or several daughters will grow pale with fear; and avoid the word 'father' unless you wish to see some of the little ones creep under the table to hide," wrote Lady Henry in *Beauty for Ashes*.

In the safe and loving environment at Duxhurst, the children's trust in adults was gradually restored. They welcomed visitors to the Nest. They enjoyed the support of local farmers who would bring sweets at Christmas time. They also delighted in letters from well-wishers, including from the secretary of the NSPCC who wrote to each child referred by the charity on their birthday. A cot could be endowed for just £10 a year.

A Duxhurst postcard. Courtesy of Richard Cooper

The Nest was a long, low building near the entrance to the village, surrounded by meadow and a pine wood at the rear. Inside, Lady Henry tells us, there was "a big, bright room, with rows of tiny chairs and little green stools, four windows with little blue curtains, a big blue dresser covered with white plates and mugs, a shelf of story-books, a rocking-horse, and a strange beast that the children call a rocking-sheep." There was also a night nursery "with rows of little blue beds" and another room with babies' cots "all in a row."

In 1913, the Nest housed twenty four girls and seven boys. They became the sons and daughters of the village, for the women patients became very involved with their care and teaching. This was very much part of Lady Henry's plan. The women could not help but respond to the needs of a child. "The presence of the children speaks to the women's hearts in a way that no human voice could do. They speak to her of her own children; they remind her of her own neglect, or perhaps of something worse than neglect, and the very love and trust that she meets among the little ones who know nothing of her past, give her new hope that she may some day live to be what these children think her."

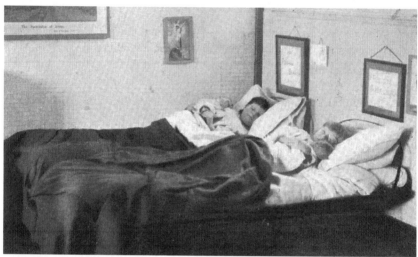

A Duxhurst postcard. Courtesy of Richard Cooper

Importantly, the children were a reminder that not everyone was at Duxhurst because they had done something wrong; they were there to "be kept good and made happy."

Before her ill-fated marriage, Lady Henry had declared a wish to have fifteen children. Although she only had one son of her own, in effect she created a second family at Duxhurst and always enjoyed spending time with the children. She would write plays for them and coach them in their lines. The first thing she would do when she returned to Duxhurst, having been staying in London or visiting elsewhere, would be to change into her simple grey uniform and go to visit her 'boys and gels'.

Lillian Brown recalls her "looking beautiful but just like all her staff" and tells how she encouraged her own grandsons to join in games with the children.

Lady Henry Somerset at Duxhurst. Photograph courtesy of Audrey Ward.

Sometimes the children were invited to spend an afternoon playing and picnicking at Reigate Priory. They would walk there, taking turns to carry a heavy laundry basket filled with special treats the cook had prepared. Other days there would be picnics in the Duxhurst fields, which Lady Henry would join whenever possible.

At one stage children of school age were taken each day to the County School in Horley. The older ones were trained in household duties and found positions with local families or with friends and supporters of Lady Henry or other staff. The evenings had a regular routine – sewing and darning, reading and choir practice.

Lady Henry is seated holding a cup of tea.

A watercolour painting of the Nest by Mary Ward Poole, friend of Lady Henry Somerset, which was made into a postcard.

The children were always welcomed back after they had moved on from the security of Duxhurst. Indeed, at least one girl returned to be married there in the little church, bringing much delight to staff and patients alike.

In 1920, the Nest burnt down, the first of many tragic fires to blight the Duxhurst estate. Thankfully no children or staff were hurt, but it must have been a very scary time for everyone. All the children had to be rehoused in other buildings on the estate.

An appeal was launched, following Lady Henry's death in 1921, for the Nest to be rebuilt, as the insurance was insufficient to meet the cost. In 1926 a new children's home, called St Mary's, was erected on the same site, although the new building was smaller and set further back from the lane at a different angle.

MEANINGFUL OCCUPATION

Upper class women often turned to drink through boredom, asserted Lady Henry, especially when their children had grown up and fled the nest. So it was important that at Duxhurst there were activities to occupy them whilst they adjusted to sobriety.

The common occupations of laundry work and cleaning were not deemed suitable for such ladies; horticulture was. A lady gardener, who had been trained at Swanley College, was recruited to manage the extensive gardens, orchards and glasshouses at Duxhurst. Whilst it was mainly the working class women who tended them, patients of the Manor House could often be found alongside them, learning new skills and acquiring an appreciation of nature previously unknown to them.

The Friends' Garden, photograph courtesy of Ideal Home Magazine

The gardens surrounding The Cottage were a rich profusion of flowers; roses and delphiniums vying for position. The Friends' Garden,

Swedish Looms. Beauty for Ashes

behind The Cottage, was the place where guests were taken to admire the blooms and to pick some flowers to remind them of their visit.

Summer time was particularly busy, with tomatoes and cucumbers to be grown, then packed for market. Bee-keeping also proved an interesting and profitable activity, Duxhurst honey being highly-prized. Jam making and seed sorting also brought in funds.

The women from the cottages would wear rough serge aprons and straw hats as they went cheerfully about their work. They would tend the animals and manage the dairy stock, although this aspect of the village proved too expensive to continue on the large scale that staff would have liked. The women took pride in their environment; it was so very different to the grime and dirt of the streets they had left behind. Lady Henry felt it was very important for the women to be engaged on tasks new to them, with no associations with their past.

There were weaving sheds and workshops where delicate embroidered items were made. Woollen underwear and stockings were knitted. Baskets were woven. Much of the output found its way into West End stores, for Lady Henry used all her influence to gain orders. Duxhurst would take stands at major exhibitions, attracting not just income but useful publicity.

There was also the pottery, which became much sought after and was sold in Selfridges. It is still collectable today. Lady Henry herself was talented artistically. She was great friends with the artist George Frederick Watts whose second wife, Mary, was a skilled potter. It was Mary who discovered that the clay at Duxhurst was ideal for pottery and who, no doubt, advised on the whole enterprise.

Outside the Duxhurst pottery sheds

The pottery continued to operate after Lady Henry's death as The Children's Village Pottery (Duxhurst) Limited and then as The Duxhurst Village Pottery Limited but went into liquidation in 1926. The sheds and kilns were left in disrepair and no trace remains today of this former hive of creativity.

Of course, running an enterprise like Duxhurst inevitably meant there were more mundane tasks to be done – laundry, sewing uniforms and cleaning, for example. Even these chores were, whenever possible, done outside. Photographs in *Beauty for Ashes* present a picture of domestic bliss but undoubtedly the women worked hard.

Duxhurst won much admiration from the authorities. When Inspectors visited they had no hesitation in agreeing that two of the cottages should be registered reformatories under the new Inebriates Act, although they did insist these cottages should not have thatched roofs! It is likely that St Hilda's, next to the hospital, was used for this purpose.

Many women were sent from London, but Lady Henry soon came to realize that the best outcomes were achieved when patients had come to Duxhurst voluntarily. Meanwhile the London County Council was looking to set up a home of its own and visited Duxhurst where they "sought and obtained most courteous and valuable information." The result was Farmfield Hospital, which was built not far from Duxhurst itself and which opened in 1900. It too had a chapel, a picturesque flower garden with lawn and lake, vegetable gardens and even a recreation room with harmonium and piano. There was a home farm where "the better behaved" were taught butter-making and baking.

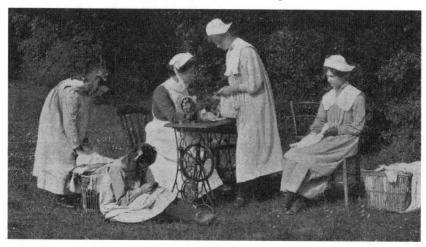

From Beauty for Ashes

St Hilda's and the hospital. Photograph courtesy of John Anthony

Somehow, the authorities had missed the point. Farmfield had much stricter discipline than Duxhurst. It was run more on prison lines. Lady Henry was not impressed. By 1913, she was writing in her diary: "Went to Farmfield with F. Oh how terrible – what a place of despair – how senseless how foolish beyond words our Public Bodies are."

A NEW LIFE

There was always a risk that when women left Duxhurst they would revert to their old ways. Some, sadly, had no home to which they could return. In such instances, Lady Henry and her staff would use all their contacts to find suitable positions for the women, preferably far away from their difficult pasts. On some occasions women were even sent to Lady Henry's own home at Eastnor Castle. Perhaps its grandeur was too overwhelming. One of Lady Henry's secretaries recounts, with some amusement, how several dinners were burnt when former Duxhurst women came as cooks but started to imbibe again.

For some women a new life in America or Canada beckoned. Many were given assisted passages, courtesy of the Salvation Army. The woman was always seen off properly. In her diary for April 1907, Lady Henry wrote about accompanying one patient from Duxhurst to Euston, where the Salvation Army special train was waiting. "I never saw anything so well organized … the band was playing well-known hymns – the bandsmen had taken an hour from their work to come here in order to put heart into the departing emigrants …"

In due course, letters would arrive at Duxhurst from across the Atlantic with reports of new beginnings. Many never forgot the help and support they had received in the village. Children too might make the epic journey. Two young boys went to work for friends of relatives of Lady Henry in Canada.

But the time was fast approaching when world events would change Duxhurst forever.

ACT 2

"Times of considerable success and days of darkness"

Father Millar who made regular visits to Duxhurst in the 1930s, describing events at the village

THE OUTBREAK OF WORLD WAR ONE

In many ways, the outbreak of the First World War brought the curtain down on Duxhurst as a rehabilitation village for inebriate women although, as we shall see, it found a new, extended role in the care of children.

Clearly the war meant that there were different, more pressing priorities not just for the government but for the philanthropists and general public.

Most urgent was the need for hospitals and convalescent homes for wounded soldiers. There is a note in the Register of Services for St Mary and the Angels, the Duxhurst church, from the summer of 1914, stating "In mid August Duxhurst received patients from St Thomas' Hospital to make room for the wounded. On Sunday afternoons, addresses to men and women." This was within a few days of the outbreak of the war.

Then, almost a year later, the Manor House was taken over by the War Office for use as a Red Cross Hospital and many of the patients were sent away, unless they could be found work nursing the soldiers or caring for the children who remained in the village. So it was that on 25th July 1915, the Manor House became home to injured servicemen and the Reverend Bisdée took up his duties as chaplain to the Red Cross flock, as the Service Register records.

Wartime memories collected by the *Rochdale Observer* include a letter from a soldier, Sergeant E Cass, writing from Duxhurst Convalescent Hospital on 14th August 1915:

"I am pleased to say that I am improving fine and am nearly fit to 'get at 'em' again. It won't be very long before I do. This is my second time wounded; the first time was last October at Ypres ... I was hit by shrapnel in the head, arm, thigh and knee, the wound in my arm paralysing the hand. I was sent to hospital in Withington, and after treatment was discharged as quite fit. I returned to the front in March. This time I had three wounds in the right upper arm, and a most peculiar thing is that it paralysed my hand. However it is now quite all right again. Not bad eh! 7 wounds and a twice paralysed hand ..."

Clearly Sergeant Cass was another indomitable spirit who graced Duxhurst with his courage and fortitude.

Soldiers outside the shop at Duxhurst

Some temporary buildings were swiftly erected in the Manor House grounds. We know from sales particulars of the estate prepared in 1936 that a large army hut was built next to the main house. Later this was converted to provide three bathrooms with seven wash-basins and three W.C.s. In addition there were "two bedrooms and laundry and another small bedroom". Close by was an outside wash-house with copper and sink.

Wounded soldiers and young children might not be thought of as an ideal mix in a rural community, but it seems to have worked well. One child who was there at this time was Lillian Brown, whose memories were recorded in the 1980s. She said the soldiers were "all very nice men. We used to go down on Sunday afternoons for a short service of prayers and hymns, then we sat on the beds talking about our life in the home. Also they told us of their families. Some of them were very sick men but when the days were sunny we were allowed to take them out for an airing in bathchairs down the long drive with a great deal of laughter and fun about us not being able to control even a bathchair

… Nurses were always on hand. We played different games of cards, also draughts, tiddlywinks and the like …" It sounds like a mutually supportive arrangement.

Lady Henry herself would join in with recreational activities arranged for the soldiers. On one occasion she decided to leave London earlier than planned so she could attend a soldiers' concert at Duxhurst. This decision may have saved her life. For that evening her flat in Gray's Inn was hit by a bomb and suffered great damage.

As well as changing priorities, there were other reasons why the welfare of inebriate women was no longer seen as so important. One of the main causes of alcoholism, so clearly identified by Lady Henry in her book *Beauty for Ashes*, was loneliness. However the war brought work and meaningful occupation for many women and gave them a new focus in their lives. Wartime restrictions on the sale of alcohol also reduced temptation.

But Lady Henry was nothing if not flexible in her humanitarian aims. She identified the need for caring homes for the increasing numbers of illegitimate babies.

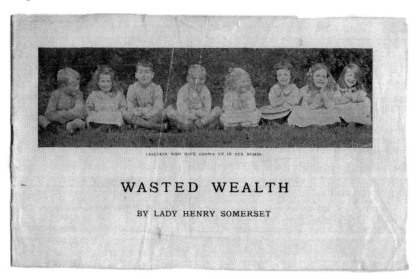

CHILDREN WHO HAVE GROWN UP IN OUR HOMES.

WASTED WEALTH

BY LADY HENRY SOMERSET

"Terrifyingly high as the death-rate is in our slums and back streets, by far the heaviest mortality is to be found among the children of unmarried mothers; and the reasons are not far to seek. Before the war such children were placed with foster mothers. Some of these women were efficient and some indifferent, but, as they are now obliged to register, they are on the whole fairly satisfactory. Since the war the foster mother is practically extinct. Work is plentiful and well paid, the rise in the cost of living has necessarily made the prices charged by them as prohibitive, and, for the most part, they will no longer accept the responsibility of the care of infants when more remunerative and more congenial work is opening everywhere. The result is that during the years of the war when more such babies have been born, the death-rate has gone up with alarming rapidity."

This work with young children won Lady Henry further critical acclaim. The *Illustrated War News* ran a continuing feature about 'Women in the War' and in January 1918 described the valuable work at Duxhurst: "Away on the windswept Surrey hills a woman is carrying on work as important as any of her sex have undertaken during the war … the babies colony started and maintained by Lady Henry Somerset is an object-lesson in child welfare that the State would do well to copy."

The article talks about how "wastage of life in the war has helped to bring realisation of the value of life" and that young children need to be healthy and strong to face the future. It praises the fact that Lady Henry expected each mother to contribute to the cost of her child's upkeep and said, "There is a fine humanity about the decision which allows such mothers who wish to be near their children to take work in the home where they are cared for. Of course, such a scheme costs money, but it only needs ten pounds a year to secure health and happiness for a baby at Duxhurst, and no one can deny that it's cheap at the price."

As the Babies Haven was established at Duxhurst, Violet's story begins, a story which spans over ninety years.

VIOLET'S STORY

As England faced the threat of Hitler's bombs, Violet Anthony knew there was just one place where she and her young family would feel safe.

Refusing all offers of help from the authorities keen to evacuate children from the London area, Violet turned to Duxhurst, her childhood home. She looked back on her early life there with great fondness. She had kept in touch with many of the friends she had made there and she knew Miss Cass, former Superintendent of Duxhurst village, still lived there. In difficult times, Duxhurst was calling Violet back.

So she wrote to Miss Cass, asking if there was any where on the estate where she and her two children might stay. Today, over seventy years later, Miss Cass' reply is still treasured by Violet. Poignantly, on the back of the envelope, Violet has written "The turning point of my life".

In the letter, Miss Cass offers Violet a safe refuge at Duxhurst, in the house of her recently widowed chauffeur Frank Wood. She clearly has great sympathy for the young family, especially with the baby hating the sight of a gas mask: " … and I don't blame him," Miss Cass writes with feeling.

Violet was just seven months old when, early in 1917, she was sent to Duxhurst. She has a small faded photograph of a woman from Arundel whom she believes was her mother. She never knew her father.

Violet is the only person I have been privileged to meet who had actually met Lady Henry Somerset. She remembers several occasions when Lady Henry was at Duxhurst, including a Christmas party in December 1920, just two months before her death. The party was held in the hall on the village green and Lady Henry took time to talk to all the children. Violet says she was a lovely lady – "Beautiful, even though she was old" and "comfortable" or "plump", a description Lady Henry herself would have enjoyed. Like all the children, Violet seems to have felt very at ease in the lady's presence. "We were never nervous or afraid of her," she recalls.

Violet's precious letter from Miss Cass

She also remembers the Reverend Russell who used to come down from London to visit Lady Henry and conduct services in the church.

Violet had not realised that he was a cousin of Lady Henry's but she thought he was a lovely man (though perhaps not as wonderful as the Reverend Lavis who came later - Violet admits to having had a bit of a crush on him!)

It is possible that Violet is one of the babies who feature in the booklet *Wasted Wealth*, written by Lady Henry Somerset in 1917. Scrubbed up and smiling, the babies look angelic, pulling at the heartstrings of possible benefactors. For Violet was there when the Nest became the Babies Haven, a refuge for illegitimate or orphaned youngsters, at a time when, in Lady Henry's own words: "more babies died than men were killed at the Front: eleven every hour, all through the year".

On the wagon. The caption, Lady Henry's own, is perhaps an ironical nod to the previous use of the village as a home for inebriate women.

Violet may well have been in the first intake of babies to Duxhurst. In *Wasted Wealth*, Lady Henry says, "The poor little mothers brought them, and, indeed, the twenty-one that came that day were a sad sight, the babies wailed, and the mothers cried at the thought of parting from that little being, the love of which was already woven in the warp of her heart. I was glad to see how much they cared. Many had brought little bundles of finely stitched clothes which they had probably made in the late hours after they had finished their work, when no one was there to wonder or to question."

BABY'S OPEN-AIR BATH.

Lady Henry goes on to say that many of the mothers came from "good service" and had been of "good character" until that "fatal moment when her young man was going away, and promised to come back and marry her" but met his death before he could do so.

Each mother had to take some financial responsibility for her child and find a guarantor for the payment of five shillings a week. Violet believes that someone in Scotland paid towards her keep at Duxhurst and she has always believed this was something to do with her father, although she is not sure how she knows this. It is possible that the Scottish benefactor was in fact a "Cot-Auntie", a kindly individual who had agreed to sponsor a particular child at Duxhurst and to send him or her birthday and Christmas cards.

Occasionally, the mothers themselves would remain at Duxhurst, where they were found work, sometimes even in the Babies Haven. It was hoped that mother and child might, in the future, be found positions and homes together.

In 1917, the year Violet arrived at Duxhurst, there were some five hundred and thirty four applications for the Babies Haven. How lucky Violet was to have been given a place. According to Lady Henry's account, these applications "come to us by letter, telegram and telephone – applications not only from the mothers themselves, but from sixty hospitals and institutions, entreating us to take infants, as they did not know how or where to care for them ..."

It clearly pained Lady Henry to have to turn any child away. Her hope was to raise sufficient funds so that more babies could be taken into the sanctuary of Duxhurst.

The first intake would, in due course, pass into the Duxhurst Children's Village, as she now called it "where we already have our own nursery school, and school for older children", thus making room for more babies in the Haven.

"I have found the inestimable benefit of keeping both girls and boys with us until they are old enough to go out into the world to earn their living – of making our Village a place to which all their lives the children look back on as a dear home where they found protection, happiness and love."

Photographs from Wasted Wealth leaflet, in which an article by Lady Henry Somerset from The Ladies' Field of December 1917 was reprinted.

Violet Anthony, Easter 2011.
Photograph courtesy of John Anthony.

Violet's story is proof that Lady Henry succeeded in her aim. In fact, were the Duxhurst project still in existence today, this lovely lady would be its best advertisement.

From an article in *The British Journal of Nursing* on September 8th, 1917, we gain a clear picture of how the Babies Haven operated. The Red Cross had finished their work treating wounded soldiers at the Manor House and so this large property was used for the babies. The room where the babies were washed and dressed was on the ground floor, "a charming room in tones of blue and white." There were three night nurseries "with delightful cots" and a sick room in case isolation to prevent infection was necessary, although each baby had to be certified as infection-free before they were accepted at Duxhurst. The writer of the article had recently visited and was charmed by the sight of all the babies in their wicker cots, forty in number, on the lawn in front of the house. "The ever-recurring problem of the provision of shoes and socks for so large a family does not trouble those in charge of the babies. It has been solved by leaving the feet free as nature intended, and shell pink toes curl about with no ill-fitting shoes to compress them and cause trouble in after-years."

The Matron, a Miss Olive Goddard, was a Queen's nurse and qualified midwife with a wealth of experience. Her staff included a Day Sister and a Night Sister, two hospital trained nurses, three nursery nurses and one nurse maid, as well as domestic staff. The babies were cared for in groups of eight, each like a small family. A typical day is described thus: "The day begins with the babies' breakfast at 7 o'clock, washing going on in another room meanwhile. Lunch is at 10 a.m., after which, on fine days, they spend the greater part of the time in the open air; dinner is at

12 o'clock, tea at 3.30, bathing begins at 4.30 p.m. and supper is at 6. The bottle babies are fed three-hourly."

It is interesting to read the 'professional' view of bottle feeding, as prevailed at the time and expressed in *The British Journal of Nursing* article: "Only whole milk is used. It may be modified to the extent that cream is removed from it or added to it, but no other modification of any kind is employed, and the babies thrive on the pure milk supplied by the Duxhurst cows – shorthorns for the most part."

One of the estate houses was used for a similar, but separate project, also under Miss Goddard's watchful eye. Patients from a London hospital came with their babies to convalesce at St Anne's Cottage at Duxhurst.

Where she had once been a leading expert on the causes of inebriety, licensing laws and the density of licensed premises in any given area, Lady Henry now made herself into an expert of child care. She consulted specialists and read widely on the matter. Her sister, Adeline, Duchess of Bedford, was also keenly interested in this work and in 1919 it was in fact Adeline who chaired the Select Committee on Child Adoption. Lady Henry gave evidence, alongside representatives from such large institutions as Barnardo's, the Salvation Army and the Church Army. The report of the Select Committee describes the work at Duxhurst as caring initially for "about sixty eight babies of about two weeks old in a separate house before they are passed into nurseries until they reach school age, school being part of the system of the colony. Over 260 babies have also been received with their mothers at St Anne's Cottage after their confinement in Queen Charlotte's Hospital."

With her knowledge and experience, Lady Henry felt able to state her firm views on adoption, which accorded with the findings of the Select Committee, that adoption should only be done in exceptional circumstances and should be regulated by the state. So were there any adoptions of children at Duxhurst? From Lady Henry's evidence, it appears there may have been a few: "In certain cases this method [adoption] of dealing with a child is deemed desirable, but it is used in the most sparing manner and chiefly connected with conditions created in married homes through the absence of the soldier husband."

As Violet grew from baby to toddler to healthy youngster, she recalls living in various of the buildings at different times, and has vague memories of the Nest burning down. At one stage she was housed in a large dormitory in the Manor House but then they moved into the cottages (boys on the left, girls on the right). This was probably about 1928 when High Trees School moved to the Manor House when their own school at Salfords burnt down. See *The High Trees School Episode*.

Despite her years, Violet can recall with great fondness the names of many of her friends from those early Duxhurst days: Jimmy, Benny, Effie with her elder sister Winnie, Mercy and Minnie. She stayed in touch with many of them for years.

The Children's Village

Jimmy was a particularly interesting character. He was a foundling, discovered on the morning of St James' Day, so he was named by Duxhurst staff 'James Morning'. He never married, telling Violet that he didn't feel it would be right to do so as he never knew who his parents were. He was proud to serve his country in the Second World War after which he became a telephone operator before retiring to a park home in Kingswood. With help from Violet's son, he managed to get a passport so he could accompany Violet on a trip to Australia to visit her daughter who had emigrated there. But he didn't want to go a second time; he missed England.

Jimmy Morning, a fine young man. Photographs courtesy of Violet Anthony.

Ethel (Effie) and Winnie were sisters, their mother, Emma, an alcoholic. She and her husband had been landlords of The Fawn public house in Deal and had six children. One of the stories passed down the family and recounted to me by Ethel's son Brian was of a raid on The Fawn by excise officers who had been tipped off about a stash of contraband brandy, newly arrived from France. The excise officers searched the premises, but found nothing. There was just one place left to look – the bedroom. But when they entered they were faced with the sight of Emma, in bed, breast feeding baby Ethel. They retreated in embarrassment, little realising that the brandy was hidden under the bedclothes. Whether Emma herself was a patient at Duxhurst at any time is unclear.

The two sisters were sent to Duxhurst in 1914, when Winnie was about eight and Ethel two. Winnie became a" little mother" to her sister, Ethel and to many of the other youngsters, including Violet. When Winnie left Duxhurst, having been found a job in Reigate by Miss Cass, she couldn't settle and returned for a while to help look after the children in the village. Eventually she did move out and then had her own family.

Ethel too enjoyed the sanctuary of Duxhurst and retained her love of the countryside throughout her life. She knew the name of every wildflower, a legacy from time spent enjoying the rural setting of Duxhurst. She

Winnie and Ethel growing up at Duxhurst. Photographs courtesy of Brian Brown, Diana Rose and Jane Bushell.

wasn't so fond of the food there though. Her children remember her talking about stew day on Wednesdays, when the meat would be mainly fat. Ethel would pick out the fat, roll it up her knicker leg then feed it to the birds later. When Ethel left Duxhurst she went to join her mother, who by this time was working for a naval officer, Commander Hardy, at his estate in Horsted Keynes. Later, she moved back to Deal where she married and had two children. Both Winnie and Ethel stayed in touch with Violet and were later to reunite to save some of the contents of the Duxhurst church from further vandalism.

It might seem surprising to see a dog in this photograph but actually there was both a village dog and a village cat at various times. Violet remembers how upset the children were when Towser, a terrier, got run over on the main road.

Winnie and Ethel

58

Many of Violet's memories are linked in some way to the church. The ceremonial form of the services appealed greatly to her, as did the music. In their free time, the children would act out their own services, wafting around old cocoa tins on string as pretend incense burners. Jimmy was always the priest and Benny the altar boy. The girls sang the hymns, *All Things Bright and Beautiful* being a particular favourite. Violet is very proud of the fact that she was in the church choir and still treasures an old hymn book. She recalls wearing a white veil and gown and sitting to one side of the nave, up by the altar.

There is a vivid account of the church written in 1981 by John Norsworthy, who had been head master of High Trees School from 1965 to the time of its closure in 1984.

Interior of St Mary and the Angels. Photograph from Beauty for Ashes

"This small building enshrined Lady Henry's ideas of heaven. She herself painted the angels about the chancel arch." There was a small porch in front of a green gothic-style door. On entering, one would pass between two canopied stalls, originally intended for the Sister Superior and the Lady Superintendent. "The sanctuary itself glowed with a strangely luminous richness, the Archangels (including Raphael, the healer) upon the apsidal end wall seeming to be figured in shallow relief. Before them was the high altar with its six candles and with two more on the credence table. Otherwise the sanctuary ... was bare of furniture, save for a draped lectern, benches of green wood round the side-walls for the servers, a prie-dieu for the priest for saying his offices, and a Glastonbury chair for his use during the Sung Mass. And, wonder of wonders, there were roses – growing up the trellis which separated the sanctuary on the gospel side from the room behind the Lady altar which housed the organ."

No wonder Violet and the other young children were enchanted, rather than overwhelmed. No wonder they loved the beautiful theatre of the services, with the dramatic 'costumes': lace-edged surplices and cassocks with matching gloves, slippers and skullcaps for the altar boys or servers, white veils and dresses for the choir girls, richly adorned chasubles and copes of the ministers. Just imagine, through a child's eyes, the glorious sight each Good Friday when the great crucifix was processed solemnly round the village. Attending services twice on Sundays were no hardship for a child like Violet. It was fun.

When the time came for Violet to be confirmed, there was not a sufficient number of candidates for the Bishop to come down from London so she travelled by coach to London, with her friend Mabel Millard accompanied by Miss Cass. The service was probably conducted at St Alban's Church in London, which was effectively Lady Henry's home church and where her cousin, the Reverend Russell officiated. Violet only remembers it as a grand adventure and not returning home to Duxhurst until midnight.

Not surprisingly Violet also remembers the sweet shop at Duxhurst. Lady Henry had struggled to raise funds for a village shop. In her book, *Beauty for Ashes*, written in 1913 she is appealing for £250 "To build what is urgently needed, a small shop for providing the little necessaries that the women are constantly requiring."

Eventually this shop was built but with the onset on the First World War it sold fewer women's necessaries and more sweets and cigarettes. It became a hub both for the soldiers recuperating in the Red Cross hospital and the children remaining in the village.

How did the children get their money for sweets, you may wonder? Violet recounts that at one time the matrons dispensed two pence per week to each child. One penny was put aside immediately for savings. The children got a stamp on a card and when they had saved a shilling, they went to the Post Office to put it into a savings account. Thus every child, on leaving Duxhurst, would have a little nest-egg of their own to help them on their way. Of the remaining one penny, half went into the church collection and the other precious half they could spend on sweets. There were ways the children could earn more. Scrubbing the kitchen floor might yield three pence; cleaning windows the rich prize of six pence. But Violet hated doing the windows.

After Lady Henry's death, it was Miss Cass who took on responsibility for the welfare of the children. She "sort-of adopted us" says Violet. She ensured each child received a good education in the village school, with great emphasis on the 3 'Rs'. Violet's favourite was writing and she would happily write her letters, perhaps to that Cot Auntie who sponsored her, each Sunday.

But Violet was a spirited girl. She loved to go off and explore the estate and often got into trouble for not being where she should be. The primroses in the woods held a particular fascination and she would always be bringing back bunches to go into jam jars in the cottage she shared with other girls. Once she became frightened when she was off exploring and came across a man sitting on a log, smoking a pipe, and she fled back to the safety of the village centre.

Although Miss Cass was never cruel, she was obviously firm. Naughty girls would be sent off to their rooms on their own to reflect on their misdoings. Violet thinks she might have been able to stay longer at Duxhurst if she had been more docile but when she was fourteen she was found a place in service in London.

She became a 'tweeny maid', a maid who assisted both the cook and the housemaid, or "dogsbody" as Violet describes it. The seven-storey house in Belgrave Square was home to an elderly spinster who was virtually bed-ridden. Ironically, there was a pub at ground floor level.

*Frank Wood around 1945. Photograph
courtesy of Violet Anthony.*

Each month, Violet would return to Duxhurst, taking sweets for the children. She always loved these visits.

It was while in service in Belgrave Square that she met her future husband, John Thomas Anthony (Tom) who had come down from the north on the famous Jarrow March. He was working as a labourer on the road outside.

Within a few years the couple were settled in Hanwell, West London and had two young children. Then the onset of World War Two saw Tom go off to fight for his country and Violet desperate to find a safe haven for her children. So she wrote that fateful letter to Miss Cass.

Violet flourished back at Duxhurst. She found Frank Wood, Miss Cass's long-serving chauffeur to be a kind man. Her son used to call Frank 'Grandad'. Violet remained living in his house until he died in 1964. Shortly after the war ended, her marriage broke down and her husband returned to the north. She later became housekeeper for Miss Withers and only finally left Duxhurst in 1987.

Frank Wood's house was on the fringe of the Duxhurst estate, off Ironsbottom. It was one of a pair of brick and slate cottages and had three bedrooms. Downstairs there was a parlour, kitchen, scullery with sink and a wash-house. Though life in wartime Britain was not easy, at least at Duxhurst Violet and her children did not go short. Violet worked hard, keeping house for Mr Wood, cleaning for Miss Cass and even working shifts at the White Hut transport café on the main road. Frank Wood had a large, productive garden and grew plenty of vegetables to see them through the year. Rabbits were caught as required, the estate orchards yielded abundant fruits.

Violet's son John (known as Tommy) enjoyed the freedom, as a young lad, to roam the lanes and woods. Unlike his mother, he never felt at ease with Miss Cass, intimidated by her severe, haughty expression, her dark hair pinned up tightly. He remembers going to The Cottage where Miss Cass lived but he was never allowed in the "new wing" as the 1919 extension was known. This had a tiled roof and compared to the other, more simple cottages in the village, it was palatial. Moreover, it had a very modern bathroom!

He remembers Canadian forces being at Duxhurst for a while during the war. The remnants of their small parade ground and assault course can still be traced just off Duxhurst Lane, close to where the village green used to be.

When Italians living in England were interned in 1941, many were placed at Duxhurst and some were allowed to work on local farms. Maureen Cole (née O'Donoghue), whose family lived on the fringe of the estate, remembers her mother one day finding two of the internees leaning on her gate. They were surprised when she spoke to them in Italian, for she had recognised their language. They subsequently came to work at her father's stables.

But this idyllic place was not immune to the ravages of war. Surrey suffered many bombings and casualties. The airfields of Croydon, Redhill, Kenley and Biggin Hill attracted enemy attention. The terrifying sound of the flying bombs, or doodlebugs as they became known, is still remembered today. Between June 16th and September 7th 1944, two hundred and ninety five of them fell in Surrey alone.

Violet's son had clearly inherited his mother's work ethic. Even when quite small, he found work on the farm or helping Mr Wood in his garden. He did milk deliveries for Miss Withers, who by this time owned Duxhurst Farm as well as Wray's Farm and Wray's Dairy and who lived nearby at Crutchfield Brae.

Violet's second stay at Duxhurst had truly transformed her life. Her indomitable spirit still shines through in the twinkle in her eyes today. Like many of her age, she can't recall what she had for breakfast but she can recall those happy days at Duxhurst and she gives thanks to Lady Henry Somerset, Gertrude Cass and Frank Wood for their kindness and generosity.

THE HIGH TREES SCHOOL EPISODE

From 1928 to 1930, High Trees School was operating from the Duxhurst estate.

This school had been founded in 1922 and originally occupied a property in Newhouse Lane, Salfords just a few miles to the east of Duxhurst. Its founder, Edith Marie Tucker, was another of those energetic and philanthropic women who have passed across the Duxhurst stage.

High Trees school was described as a Children's Convalescent Home or "For Children in need of country air". According to *High Trees School: the History of a school near Horley* written by Brian Buss and Richard Cooper of the Horley Local History Society in 2002, it met a very real need as a boarding school for children following the First World War. The fathers were often too wounded to support their families and the mothers had to work; some parents were working abroad in countries like India. Some placements were for short periods, others for longer.

Miss Tucker and Miss Young at Selsey.
Photograph courtesy of Richard Cooper

Miss Tucker was assisted in her work by Miss Ethel May Young who took responsibility for the educational needs of the children.

The two women clearly believed in the benefits of fresh air, exercise and country living. The boys and girls would be walked to Outwood Common for picnics. Chickens and other animals were kept. In August, the school would decamp to the coast at Selsey.

Then in March 1928, disaster struck. A great fire raged through the school and despite the efforts of the staff, five children died. Miss Young, who personally saved three children, Miss Tucker and Miss Parry (another member of staff) were awarded certificates for their bravery. The tragedy made the front page of the national newspapers and offers of help and support flowed in from around the country. In the local area, people rallied round. The Monotype Corporation in Honeycrock Lane, Salfords, immediately offered practical assistance, providing breakfast and lunch for children and staff in their canteen for several days.

Desperate for new accommodation, Miss Tucker turned towards Duxhurst. She knew that the Manor House there was under-utilised and that the owners were desperate for cash to keep the village going. So she arranged to rent the Manor House together with two other houses, St Agnes and St Christophers and the school quickly became operational in its new home.

In many ways, Miss Tucker's philosophy of childcare matched that of Duxhurst's founder, Lady Henry Somerset. Clearly the rural environment of Duxhurst was ideal for the outdoor activities which were such an important part of High Trees School life.

High Trees children play outside the Manor House.

Empire Day celebrations at Duxhurst. Photographs courtesy of Richard Cooper.

The school flourished at Duxhurst and by its second year there, more accommodation was required so two of the cottages around the village green were then also rented. At times, there were almost fifty children at the school, with up to ten babies. Day pupils were admitted for the first time in January 1930.

The memories of former pupils of this period are recorded in *High Trees School: a History of a School near Horley*: "Some remembered those two years very fondly. The garden was said to be so large and magnificent. There was a huge lawn and massive rhododendron bushes in clumps that you could chase your friends around and not find them. There was a vast pond and beautifully kept hedges everywhere. Before breakfast on most mornings the children walked four times round the large lawn that was said to equal one mile. In the summer lessons were held in the garden sitting at green folding chairs and desks that were always having to be moved to shadier spots."

High Trees School had clearly brought new life and vigour to Duxhurst village. The school children would attend the village church on Sundays and they would keep their chickens, goats and other animals in the grounds.

However, the school was only a paying tenant and throughout its two years at Duxhurst, Miss Tucker was constantly on the look-out for a more permanent home. By February 1930, she had purchased a large property nearby at Horse Hill, which included a main house, a cottage and stables, which were quickly converted to rooms. By the end of July 1930, the school had moved out of Duxhurst.

There is a wonderful memory of this move captured in *High Trees School: a History of a School near Horley:*

"Every child who had a bicycle or tricycle or scooter or pram to push, got under way and the whole School took to the road. There were very few cars in those days and just as well, as I remember we were three or four abreast and certainly too excited to heed any appeals for caution."

The new school at Horse Hill. Photograph courtesy of Richard Cooper

The new High Trees School at Horse Hill flourished in its new home for another fifty years, whilst Duxhurst's fortunes declined.

GERTRUDE MARGARET CAREW CASS, SUCCESSOR TO LADY HENRY SOMERSET

Lady Henry Somerset had been constantly worried about money and the cost of running such a large enterprise as Duxhurst became. Over the years she frequently wrote in her diary, quoted in Kathleen Fitzpatrick's 1923 biography, expressing her concerns and frustrations:

Jan 5, 1907: "Oh how condemned I am at my past extravagance now. I should have had money to help out."

Jan 23, 1913: "Money matters very trying and unrestful. I want to do right but always seem to have managed to do wrong."

And even as late as Dec 20, 1919: "I have had a time of much care and worry ... Money, money, always the same dull refrain ... the abiding feeling – it is my own fault, my bad management."

Yet few people could have done more to raise the necessary funds for Duxhurst than Lady Henry did.

There had been some generous benefactors and supporters: Mrs Massingbred, a temperance stalwart, Lady Somers, Isabel's mother who paid much of the cost of building the Nest, and her sister, Adeline, Duchess of Bedford, who at one stage paid off a £3,000 building debt. Her son, Somers Somerset, although willing to be one of several Trustees, must have quaked at the idea of taking on such a huge liability for the future.

However, at a time when both financial and managerial support was sorely needed, a wealthy lady arrived at Duxhurst, possibly initially as a patient herself, Gertrude Margaret Carew Cass. In due course, Miss Cass became Deputy Superintendent and on Isabel's death in 1921, she fought hard to keep Duxhurst going, especially the work of the Children's Village. She bought much of the land, with a mortgage, before Isabel died. She took over Isabel's house, The Cottage, on a long term lease at a peppercorn rent.

When the late John Norsworthy wrote his history of Duxhurst in 1981, entitled *Beauty to Ashes* after Lady Henry Somerset's own book about the village, he had been able to make contact with various people who still remembered the later years of the village, including several clergymen

Gertrude Cass. Photograph courtesy of Violet Anthony.

who had been involved with Duxhurst at various stages.

Father Blagdon-Gamlen told him about Father Alban Henry Baverstock, who was director of the Holy Family Homes Incorporated for a while in the 1930s. He quotes from a letter received from Father Baverstock in 1944: "I had a trying experience at Duxhurst where I spent two years (1930 -1932) as, nominally, Priest Director of the Holy Family Homes there, but actually was thwarted in all I wanted to do by the Committee which sat in London and listened to any ill-natured story which came from difficult people on the spot; their secretary was mismanaging their finances, and they were heading for the bankruptcy in which they were afterwards involved. I left it – it was all that I could do".

It would seem that Miss Cass stepped in at this point, using some of her own money to keep Duxhurst afloat. At this time she was still a wealthy woman. John Norsworthy records her gardener Mr Luckin saying how she drove around in a very smart car and visited Bournemouth regularly.

To bail out Duxhurst, she sold some of her mining shares to realise funds. Sadly, following nationalization, her remaining shares became almost worthless and her income from them significantly reduced, so she died in straitened circumstances.

We know very little of Miss Cass's background. Her obituary in The Times in March 1958 states that she was the "daughter of a Middlesex clergyman, who insisted that she should have the same education by tutor as was given to his sons." One of her brothers may also have become a parson. She was certainly a very religious person and when she moved into The Cottage she kept all the icons and imagery that adorned it, probably even adding more of her own. This is very apparent from photographs of the house printed in 1923 in *The Ideal Home Magazine*.

From her obituary, we learn that during the First World War, Miss Cass set up a convalescent home for officers in Worthing, receiving an O.B.E. in recognition of this charitable endeavour. She was also listed in the London Gazette of 30th March 1920 as "Donor, Commandant and Matron of Molant War Hospital, Brockenhurst."

Of course, trying to follow in Lady Henry's footsteps was a tall order. Some of the children who had been at Duxhurst in the early 1920s recalled that she was quite strict, perhaps not quite as readily forgiving as her predecessor.

Certainly Lillian Brown, who had lived at Duxhurst between 1912 and 1923, did not like her. Lillian, having been brought up in the village since she was eight, felt herself very privileged when, at the age of fifteen, she was given the position of tweeny maid at The Cottage. She loved Lady Henry, recalling that if any member of staff treated the children there harshly, they would be dismissed as soon as her mistress found out about the matter. However, when Miss Cass took over, Lillian found her "a very hard person to please." She claims Miss Cass did not pay her any wages for two years, just provided board and lodging. "According to her I had no name. She always called me 'that girl'". When Lillian handed in a month's notice, Miss Cass demanded that she leave straight away, even though she had not at that stage secured an alternative position.

But as Violet Anthony's story shows, there was a very kindly, generous side to Miss Cass as well. Indeed, it was lovely to hear the Duke of Beaufort, Lady Henry's great grandson, recall being taken, as a boy, to visit Miss Cass at Duxhurst. He enjoyed these occasions, especially the fact that as he left Miss Cass would give him a shilling. Staff were very loyal to her and many, like her chauffeur Frank Wood, stayed in her employment all their lives.

In her later years, Miss Cass was a friendly neighbour. Brothers Barry and Tony Morgan lived from 1954 to 1960 in Somerset Cottage, next door to The Cottage. They remember going to tea with Miss Cass and found her very kind and very pleasant, in a wizened sort of way. She had the manners and speech of someone high-born but enjoyed having children round to visit, with or without their mother.

The Morgan brothers also remember Miss Cass's friend, Miss Graham, and the housekeeper, Mrs England, with much fondness. They were struck by all the religious imagery around the house but felt this was important to Miss Cass.

Gina and Peter Knox remained friendly with Gertrude Cass right up until her death. Gina recalls visiting her in The Cottage when she was very frail, almost ghost like, shrouded in white bedding. She spent a period during her later years in a nursing home in Reigate.

Miss Cass's funeral service, following her death, aged ninety nine, on 14th March 1958, was held at Emmanuel Church, Sidlow and was attended by many local people, including her chauffeur Frank Wood. This was followed by her burial in the tiny churchyard of St Mary and The Angels at Duxhurst, close by where she had lived for much of her life. Today Gertrude Cass's gravestone is forgotten, the engraving fading. Yet, like her friend Lady Henry Somerset, her generosity had made a great difference to many people's lives.

Dining room of The Cottage. Photograph courtesy of Ideal Home Magazine

DIFFERENT NAMES, SAME PLACES

One of the challenges in researching the history of Duxhurst has been the constant change in names of many of the buildings in the village; indeed the whole village at various times was known by different names as different benefactors and charitable organisations became involved: The Homes of the Holy Redeemer, The Lady Henry Somerset Homes, the Holy Family Homes to give but a few examples. After Lady Henry's death, Miss Cass let part of the village to Princess Marie Louise for her Homes for Poor Gentlewomen. It is not clear whether this was the same enterprise as the Friends of the Poor, which rented part of the site from 1926 to provide a home for old women.

This delightful drawing of Somerset Cottage was done by Arthur Hutchinson for the Morgan family in 1960.

But at the core, there was always the Manor House, the cottages either side of the village green, the recreation hall at the head of the horseshoe, the church, the children's home and the hospital.

If Lady Henry Somerset decided there was a particular need she could meet at Duxhurst, even if it would only be for a short period, she would try to make accommodation available. Hence we hear that St Monica's cottage was used for a short time by a group of twelve girls, aged about fifteen, who came to be trained for laundry work rather than being sent to a remand home. These girls were provided with a uniform of pink dresses, white aprons and white caps. They may have arrived looking rather woebegone but by the time they left Duxhurst they were a very happy and contented lot of young women, according to Lillian Brown's memoirs.

In July 1917, Duxhurst Reformatory School was certified for twelve children, then re-certified for four children at St Ursula Cottage and twenty four at Bridget Cottage. This part of the village's work ceased in August 1921.

There were also several fires during Duxhurst's life time. The Nest burnt down, as did St Agnes cottage. The fire brigade was hampered by low water pressure for their hoses, so the damage was often uncontrollable. Houses might be built on the same sites but with different names. Thus, the reincarnation of the Nest was as St Mary's.

To complicate matters further, at times there were small groups of nuns at Duxhurst, from different orders. The first, women from The Order of St Anne, stayed in St Crispins (now called Somerset Cottage), the house next to The Cottage.

It was Lady Henry's sister, Adeline, who had first brought the work of this Order to her attention. It was dedicated to the care of children in need, a natural fit for Duxhurst. The first four associates to the Order were admitted in 1917 and there were two additional novices the following year. They took increasing responsibility for the education of the children of the village. They had their own chapel on the side of their house, with a bell outside which called them to prayer. This can still be seen today, although the house has undergone many other changes.

By 1920, this community of nuns had grown in number and it was hoped to extend St Crispins and enlarge the chapel. Following Adeline's death, and in her memory, in June 1920, Lord Halifax launched an appeal for three thousand pounds to carry out this work. Talking about the work of

73

the village, Lord Halifax said, "The spirit of the place is the very opposite of all that is mechanical, institutional and coercive. Religious teaching plays a considerable part in its regenerating, educative influence."

However, shortly after Lady Henry's death the following year, these Nuns departed.

Later, nuns from the Order of the Sacred Passion came to Duxhurst. This order had been founded by Bishop Frank Weston of Zanzibar, someone well-known to Lady Henry. He was a prominent figure in the Anglo-Catholic church and had "a magnetic personality" and a "rare combination of character and intellect." If you consider his concluding address *Our Present Duty* at the Anglo-Catholic Conference in 1923, when he said "You cannot claim to worship Jesus in the Tabernacle, if you do not pity Jesus in the slum", you can see that his views very much accorded with Lady Henry's. It had been Bishop Weston who had dedicated the new aisle of the Duxhurst Church in 1914.

By the late 1920s, Duxhurst was struggling. An income of £2,000 p.a. was being received from the tenant of Duxhurst Farm, Mr Floyd Churches. The tenancy agreement included a provision that the tenant would supply, and Miss Cass would purchase, between fifteen and seventeen gallons of milk a day from cows kept at the farm, to be delivered twice daily. There were stringent conditions as to how the land was to be farmed, and a prohibition on the farmer allowing any of his labourers or others to sleep in the barns or outbuildings. Miss Cass retained shooting and sporting rights and was responsible for the structure of the farm house and other buildings included in the lease, except for the wheat thatch which the tenant had to supply. But this income was quite insufficient to keep the estate going.

Mary Ward Poole, a loyal secretary and supporter of Lady Henry Somerset's, wrote some notes which are filed in the archives at Eastnor Castle. The date of these notes is unknown, but they seem to have been written in the early 1930s, probably for the benefit of Lady Henry's cousin's wife, Verena, as both women felt strongly that Kathleen Fitzpatrick's biography *Lady Henry Somerset*, published in 1923, had not done full justice to her achievements.

From these notes we learn that The Holy Family Homes got involved in October 1929, when Father Baverstock received "a kind of S.O.S. telegram" from Miss Cass and "on going to Duxhurst found it was being closed down". The Holy Family Homes (Incorporated) described itself as doing "The Anglo Catholic Children's Work" and being supported by voluntary donations. In 1934, according to their letter heading, they had a hostel for boys in Albany Street, London, homes in Eastbourne, Weston-Super-Mare and Streatham and a 'Village', as they described The Lady Henry Somerset Homes at Duxhurst.

Following Miss Cass's appeal for help, Duxhurst was transferred to The Holy Family Homes, "an anonymous donor having freed Duxhurst from its mortgage of £14,000." There was still a debt of a further £2,500, plus the need for some urgent repairs, estimated cost around £1,000. Father Baverstock launched an appeal for further funds but it is not clear how much was forthcoming. Yet at this point, The Holy Family Homes thought they had acquired a bargain, as they believed the value of the property to be "a tremendous asset – estimated at about £30,000 and the furniture and fittings to about £5,000."

How wrong they were. Mary Ward Poole writes, "I have heard that Father Baverstock had nearly broken down with nervous worry over Duxhurst." For, if Holy Family Homes thought they could capitalise on the estate's value, they were very wrong. The Dorking & Horley Rural District Council were not amenable to the idea of development on the Duxhurst site. By 1932, The Holy Family Homes was trying, unsuccessfully, to sell the estate. In 1934, they were appealing to the Council "to connect the Colony with the main drainage free of cost on a first-class guarantee of interest on capital until the frontages can meet the charges." That plea fell on deaf ears.

There was confusion because under the Town Planning scheme the land had been zoned at a density of four houses to the acre but, most significantly, it was deemed not 'ripe for development' due to its lack of services. So the four houses per acre would only be relevant if, or when, the services were in place.

By September 1935 there was a definite offer on the table but the issue of drainage scuppered this again, despite a fervent plea to the Council from Mr Stanton, Secretary (and Land Agent) of The Holy Family

Homes: "I have no doubt that your council are aware that this Society is in grave financial difficulties, and that there is a heavy mortgage on the estate. It is, therefore, absolutely vital that we dispose of the property as early as possible." Mr Stanton actually lived on the estate himself, occupying St Katherine's, one of the more substantial properties.

Dorking and Horley Rural District Council responded slightly more sympathetically but it was still a 'no'. "The Council very carefully considered the zoning of this estate in view of your present difficulties but the precedence that would be caused if you were allowed to develop without restriction would completely ruin Town Planning agreements of adjacent properties and any other land so zoned ..."

The Holy Family Homes grew increasingly desperate to offload the estate. As their agents advised, any proposed sale was complicated by the fact that there were two annuities on the estate, estimated to be worth around £4,000. Their advice was to free the title from these annuities but make it subject to a life tenancy, in favour of Miss Cass, of The Cottage, two small cottages and a garage. Holy Family Homes was hoping for £25,000 from a sale free from the annuities, or £21,000 if the purchaser took over the annuities. "If we only got £20,000, this would be less than the bank overdraft and the bank might not feel disposed to release the deeds for such a sum," they complained. They were also reminded that as "one of the most attractive assets of the estate" – the Cottage – could not be sold with vacant possession but only with a reversionary interest, this too affected the value of the estate. The hard truth was that what they had paid for it was irrelevant.

There was some interest from Holborn Borough Council which was looking for a convalescent home for children. Did Lady Henry Somerset still have friends in Holborn from her time living in Gray's Inn, one wonders? This interest never came to anything.

The whole estate went to auction on 24th November 1936.

The sales particulars provide a wealth of information about Duxhurst at that time. The property was described as "A group of Domestic and Administrative buildings built and planned for institutional purposes, providing ample accommodation for over 100 persons and staff, together with about 12 acres of level ground suitable for playing fields" as well

Front page of the 1936 Auction Catalogue, courtesy of
Reigate Priory Museum

as "The Manor House, several attractive detached houses and cottages with good gardens, convenient areas of building land with good road frontages" and "A splendid Dairying and Mixed Farm, with Superior House, and Good Modernised Buildings", in all around one hundred and eighty one acres.

It was hoped to sell the estate as a whole, probably to a charity or other institution but there was provision for lots to be sold separately. However there was a stipulation that if Lot 1 failed to sell, the remaining lots would be withdrawn.

Lot 1 was the very heart of the village, the actual original colony of houses around the village green, together with the recreation hall, hospital building, village shop and post office and a level recreation and playing field.

No institutional purchaser came forward, either for the whole or for Lot 1, for many of the buildings were already showing their age. Many were said to be empty at this point in time, something which did not encourage buyers. Other buildings were let, so we see the Manor House was now let to the Universities Mission to Central Africa, the farm, several fields and two cottages still let to Mr Lloyd Churches and of course The Cottage, various other houses and two garages actually within the grounds of the Manor House, to Miss Cass for the remainder of her life at a peppercorn rent.

These sales particulars tell us what each cottage was called at that time and it is clear that over the years these names had changed around. No longer were the buildings named after the original benefactors. Now most of the cottages round the village green were named after saints: St Veronica, St Benedict, St Michael, St Margaret, St Agnes (not to be confused with another house which had at one time been called St Agnes), St Faith, St Joseph and St Dominic. Two of the cottages were named after people – the 'Emma Parker' and of course the 'Isabel Somerset'.

The two cottages which fronted the main road to Brighton, now the A217, were marketed as being "eminently suitable for use as a tea garden" because of the "enormous volume of traffic" which passed along the road. Both cottages were brick-built with slated roofs and quite substantial, each having a sitting room, kitchen and scullery and three bedrooms. One was at that time rented to a Mrs Grose for ten shillings a week. The photograph of one of these cottages in the sales particulars clearly shows the arch over the driveway into Duxhurst Village, so we know this must have still been in situ in 1936.

EMINENTLY SUITABLE FOR USE AS A TEA GARDEN.

LOT No. 5.
(Coloured Blue on Plan)

With Vacant Possession on Completion of Purchase.

LOT No. 6.
(Coloured Mauve on Plan)

With Vacant Possession on Completion of Purchase.

This Lot would make a most attractive private house, or is suitable as an adjunct to Lot 1.

THE CHILDREN'S HOME
known as

St. Mary's at Duxhurst

An attractive detached house of modern construction in brick, rough-cast, with tiled roof, occupying a delightful position, open at the front and with woodland at the back.

One of the more modern buildings, with its own central heating, on the estate at that time was St Mary's, the rebuilt children's home. This was described as "an attractive detached house of modern construction in brick, rough-cast, with tiled roof, occupying a delightful position, open at the front and with woodland at the back." Estate-agent speak hasn't altered much in the last seventy five years!

But St Mary's was a scaled-down version of the original Nest. It had just six bedrooms and one bathroom, with a separate W.C. On the ground floor it sounds more spacious, having a living room of 18ft 9ins by 17 ft, a kitchen, dining room and two other rooms.

One part of the village was described as a "Close of Pasture Land, suitable for building development". Given Holy Family Homes' discussions with the Council about development of the village, one wonders if this wasn't a bit optimistic.

The Cottage, now the home of Miss Cass and originally built as home for Lady Henry Somerset herself, was clearly superior in every way to the smaller, simple, cottages of the village centre. Its name was a misnomer, as the auction particulars made clear, calling it "a picturesque secluded country house" built of brick and timber, with a Norfolk thatched roof and eight bedrooms. The garden got a special mention. No doubt Lady Henry would have been delighted to know that her pride and joy was still described as "extremely beautiful." Miss Cass had clearly been looking after it well.

The Cottage is one of the few village buildings to remain at Duxhurst in 2011. A fuller description of it, past and present, can be found in Act 3, later in this book.

Adjacent to it is another building which is still recognisable today, although it has had several alterations and additions made to it. Then

Front and rear of Somerset Cottage in the 1950s, photographs courtesy of Tony and Barry Morgan.

known as St Crispins, it is now called Somerset Cottage. Even in 1936, it deserved its description as a "country cottage residence". It was brick built and had a partly thatched and partly tiled roof. On the left hand end was the single storey 'chapel' from when the building had been used by the nuns, although this was now a dual aspect sitting room with "lofty ceiling and wood block floor". When Peter and Gina Knox were renovating the property in the 1960s they discovered an incense burner in the roof space. In 1936, there were just three bedrooms upstairs, approached by two staircases, a clear indication that alterations had already been made to the building by this time. By the 1950s, when the Morgans rented the property, there were squirrels in the thatch. Mrs Morgan would use the chapel bell to call her two sons in for meals.

The Holy Family Homes went into liquidation in July 1939 and their homes for children, including Duxhurst, were taken over by the Homes of St Nicholas, but this appears also to have been a short term arrangement.

A new player was about to appear in the Duxhurst drama, another organization which shared many of the aims and objectives of the original Duxhurst village – the Alexandra Orphanage.

THE ALEXANDRA ORPHANAGE

The history of this body, now part of the Royal Alexandra and Albert School based at Gatton Park on the north side of Reigate, dates back to 1758 when a group of wealthy and philanthropic gentlemen set up a charitable foundation for an "Orphan Working School." The purpose of the establishment was not so much educational as vocational, to prepare the children for the workplace. The charity had some famous supporters, including Queen Victoria and William Wilberforce. By the mid nineteenth century the Orphan School was based at Maitland Park, in Haverstock Hill, North London.

In 1864, a separate charitable foundation was set up, specifically to provide homes for infants until they were old enough to attend the Orphan School. This enjoyed the patronage of Princess Alexandra, Princess of Wales, and the new project took her name, with the Alexandra Orphanage opening in 1865 in Hornsey Rise, London. Interestingly, another patron was Princess Mary, Duchess of Teck, who several years later actually carried out the official opening of Duxhurst as Lady Henry Somerset's farm colony for inebriate women.

In 1876, the Orphan School and the Alexandra Orphanage charitable foundations merged and the name Alexandra Orphanage was adopted for all its operations.

There proved to be a huge demand for places and the First World War greatly added to pressures on the charity, as more and more children were taken in. One wealthy and public-spirited Surrey family – the miller, Joseph Rank, and his sons James V. Rank (Rank, Hovis, McDougall) and J. Arthur Rank (who founded the entertainment business that became the Rank Organization) were staunch supporters of the charity. James became treasurer and a strong voice on the governing body. He lived at the time at Godstone, Surrey. In the summer he would invite all the children from the orphanage to spend a day at his home, where they enjoyed hospitality and entertainment, even being allowed to swim in the open-air swimming pool there. The 1939 Annual Report of the Alexandra

Orphanage talks of "the great pleasure of the children at leaving even for one day the streets and houses which surround the present orphanage."

Such kind-heartedness has echoes of Lady Henry Somerset, who would invite the Duxhurst children to picnics at her own country residence, Reigate Priory. The similarities did not end there, for James V. Rank was a fervent believer in the benefits of clean country air. Although the orphanage drew up plans to upgrade Maitland Park, it became clear that it was uneconomical to spend the huge sums of money required to bring the ninety year old buildings up to modern requirements. James V. Rank championed the cause of a move to Surrey.

As the Annual Report explained: "Then came the National crisis [the threat of another war], when it was brought home to the Committee very forcibly how inadvisable it was to retain a large number of children in one body in London. The idea of moving the orphanage into the country, so attractive, and so commendable for reasons of health, was now definitely supported by reasons of expediency." The neglected, but beautifully situated, one hundred and eighty acre Duxhurst estate fitted the bill perfectly.

It is fascinating to read about the plans the orphanage had for Duxhurst. Their architects, Messrs Gelder and Kitchen, designed a scheme which had separate houses, each sleeping about forty children, with a central dining hall, an assembly hall and gymnasium, a chapel, a hospital, a swimming pool, together with kitchens, bakery, workshops and offices. It was planned so that all the buildings would be built in a crescent, all facing south, on a ridge of ground which afforded a lovely view of Reigate Hill, Box Hill and the Surrey countryside. This sounds very much like an updated version of Lady Henry's original village and one wonders whether the architects were inspired by what they saw at Duxhurst when the estate was first purchased. Even though the original buildings were not suitable for refurbishment, the concept clearly was worth revisiting.

There is a strange echo in the Orphanage's 1939 Annual Report, as they appealed for money to make their ambitious plans a reality: "The planning of the estate will give an opportunity to friends who would like to name a building after someone whose memory they wish to honour." Remember those first cottages, named after the temperance branches and other benefactors who had contributed generously!

The orphanage was keen to use every contact it had for raising funds. Its president was H.R.H. the Duke of Kent. The Worshipful Company of Merchant Taylors was very supportive. Even the BBC gave air time to fund raising appeals. In January 1939 two pupils, Angela and John, both aged ten, spoke about the work of the orphanage: "There are other boys and girls who have lost their father or mother and who need someone to care for them," said John, whilst Angela talked wistfully about wanting a "new school in the country, where it will be very healthy, and a good deal safer in time of crisis." £1,310 came flooding in from listeners. Imagine how Lady Henry would have relished such an opportunity to pull at the nation's heart strings. She would surely have used the wireless, just as she used the press of her time. And in the twenty first century, she would have undoubtedly had a strong internet presence, tweeting and blogging for all she was worth.

Just as World War One changed Duxhurst forever, so World War Two changed the Alexandra Orphanage's plans. With only two hours' notice, the day after war was declared, all the children were evacuated from Maitland Park. The seniors moved to Bishopswood Park, near Reading but the juniors went to Duxhurst, where they were housed in the empty cottages. The Manor House was to be their school. Then just a few months later, Duxhurst was once again requisitioned by the army. The juniors and nursery had to move, yet again, this time to Goring-on-Thames.

Despite the war, it seemed that James V. Rank had not given up his plans for the Alexandra Orphanage at Duxhurst. His father, Joseph Rank, also a Vice-President, donated £12,000 in 1940 for the building of a new church as part of the scheme for the school's new home at Duxhurst. As a staunch Methodist, he may have been uncomfortable with the idea of the children attending the existing Duxhurst Church of St Mary and the Angels, filled as it was with Anglo-Catholic symbolism; or perhaps he was just intent on the school having its own in-house chapel. Sadly Joseph died in 1943, unaware that those plans for Duxhurst would not come to fruition.

There are indications that the orphanage tried to keep some active management of the estate during the war, at times letting Duxhurst Farm to tenant farmers. For example during 1941, the charity paid for the rebuilding of a barn which had collapsed, "a somewhat heavy outlay," but it was deemed the tenant farmer's agricultural work was "so necessary to the welfare of the nation."

As noted in the orphanage's 1942 Annual Report, "The experience of caring for the children in rural districts has been reassuring to the Board of Management, who are looking forward to the possibility after the war of carrying out the scheme of erecting new premises at Duxhurst."

In late 1943, the orphanage approached the council as they were "considering the possibility of their frontage [on the Reigate – Hookwood road] after the war and ... wishing to make provision in the lease they were now granting on the Farm, for the exclusion of certain portions of the land for development after the war." In the event, that lease for the Farm was never completed. However, the orphanage was planning ahead. A new orchard was planted the following year. Fruit from the old orchard had been sent each year from Duxhurst to the orphanage's children in their temporary accommodation.

In January 1944, the orphanage was delighted to learn that by order of the King, it would henceforth be called 'The Royal Alexandra School'.

During 1945 talks were on-going between the Royal Alexandra School and Surrey County Council's Chief Education Officer. The County Council was proposing at this stage to build a new primary school at Duxhurst for four hundred children, bringing in three hundred from surrounding districts. Older children would be catered for by secondary schools in Horley, the Grammar School in Reigate or the technical school in Redhill, with transportation provided for the Orphanage children by the County Council. The pre-war plans for Duxhurst were re-examined, but despite all efforts to identify savings, the estimated costs had risen by two thirds.

Shortly afterwards Surrey County Council suggested that the organization should consider talks with the Royal Albert School, then based in Camberley. Although, initially, the Board of Management was not keen on the idea, ultimately there was a merger in 1949.

In the midst of all this, in 1946 the Royal Alexandra School received the news that the army was about to derequisition Duxhurst. To their consternation, they discovered that the army was under instructions to offer all premises they were no longer using to the Ministry of Health for housing purposes. The Ministry in turn had offered the estate to the local authority, all without reference to the Board of the school. Duxhurst's future might have been very different if the school had not acted quickly. They successfully pleaded with the local authority to be allowed to repossess Duxhurst, so that their own plans for development of new premises could be carried out.

Within a few months they had renovated the Manor House and many of the cottages and other buildings, even installing central heating, though it was hoped that much of the heating apparatus could be recycled into the new premises in due course. Some of the cost was met by a grant for dilapidations made by the army.

"In making arrangements for the reception there of the youngest members of our family every consideration has been given to their welfare, comfort and safety," the 1947 Annual Report declared.

They certainly seemed to have achieved this, for according to Gina Knox who lived in Somerset Cottage as a child at this time, the estate was beautiful, "a magical place." She remembers her mother inviting all the little girls from the orphanage to her sister's christening party and seeing all the babies in their wicker cots, tucked under red blankets.

Photograph from the Alexandra Orphanage 1947 Annual Report courtesy of The Royal Alexandra and Albert School

Children of the Alexandra Orphanage at Duxhurst. Photographs courtesy of The Royal Alexandra and Albert School.

The nursery and infants moved back to Duxhurst in February 1947 and were joined the following month by others who had been on the waiting list, bringing total numbers up to seventy seven.

The Manor House was quickly made into a school for the children. Surrey County Council made a grant towards the cost, as it was unable to find places in its local schools for such a number. But the seniors of the Royal Alexandra Orphanage never made it to Duxhurst.

With plans progressing for the merger with the Royal Albert School, a new, larger site was being sought and Gatton Park was made available to

Boys play at the back of St Mary's

the school on advantageous terms by the widow of Jeremiah Coleman, the mustard baron. The dream of a large school in idyllic rural surroundings was eventually to be realised, but not at Duxhurst.

Thankfully, a buyer, and another colourful character in the Duxhurst story, was found - Miss Alfreda Withers. Miss Withers lived and farmed locally and paid £28,000 to add the Duxhurst estate to her landholdings.

MISS WITHERS

Miss Withers was certainly a local character, recognized by everyone as she drove around the area in a big yellow van. She smoked a pipe and usually dressed as a man, often being seen in a trilby or a suit and tie, although she did wear a skirt when she attended the local Catholic church in Horley. She never sought to hide the fact that she had a female partner, a Miss Lord.

Miss Withers. Photograph courtesy of Violet Anthony

Miss Withers' father owned several cinemas in Wales and it was he who funded the purchase of land around Duxhurst for his daughter. Perhaps he sensed the area would provide a safe refuge for her. And he was right, in that she became an accepted part of the local community, providing work for many people.

She didn't hesitate to take action though if she wanted someone to move out. Pauline Hardy's mother recalls being evicted from The Priest's House on Duxhurst Lane when her daughter was just two months old. Although the property was not in good condition (there were rats in the thatch) it was at least a home and losing it was a major problem for the young family.

Miss Withers did fall prey to exploitation when a Mrs O'Hara, who used to work in her office, embezzled some money. Mrs O'Hara had a string of previous convictions but somehow secured herself a job with Miss Withers. She would sell property she didn't own and take money for goods she never delivered, swindling many people. Eventually the law caught up with her.

When she bought the Duxhurst estate in 1949, Miss Withers would have been aware that certain parts of it were subject to a tenancy for life for Miss Cass. As Miss Cass was ninety years old at the time, Miss Withers probably didn't see this as a problem. However, Miss Cass lived to be ninety nine and it was only on her death in 1958 that Miss Withers was able to sell off properties such as The Cottage (to the Greens) and Somerset Cottage (to Gina and Peter Knox). Thus Gina was able to return to her childhood home, this time to raise her own family and, with her husband, restoring Somerset Cottage to its former glory.

As we shall see in Act 3, Miss Withers had numerous battles with the local authority, trying to get permission to knock down and redevelop the cottages in the centre of the village. Having refused permission, the council was then obliged to compulsorily purchase the land.

To some it seemed as though Miss Withers was never that interested in Duxhurst – it had been her father's idea to buy the estate. Her home remained nearby at Crutchfield Brae, so she never lived herself in the village.

However, many who knew Miss Withers well still hold fond memories of her. Gina Knox said that when she died in 1987 "she left a big hole." Violet Anthony finally moved away from Duxhurst only after Miss Withers died, as she had worked as her housekeeper for many years and had become very friendly with her family, especially Miss Wither's sister, Wendy. Indeed Violet frequently enjoyed holidays in Wales, at the Withers family's cottage in Aberporth.

Miss Withers was often reluctant to spend money on essential works to the Duxhurst properties. Yet this was just one factor which led to the dramatic decline of the village. Amazingly, as many of the properties fell into disrepair, two of the great themes of the Duxhurst drama – education and care for the disadvantaged – would continue for some time in the village.

ACT 3

"The clock on the village hall stopped years ago at 11.20
It will never tick again.
Duxhurst is dead"

News of the World 7th November 1965

THE CONTINUING MYSTERY OF THE CHURCH OF ST MARY AND THE ANGELS

How could such a lovely church, one on which Isabel Somerset had lavished such love and money, be left to fall into ruin and then effectively disappear?

This is a question which has fascinated me since I first learnt the story of the Duxhurst Village.

When there is no person or body with clear ownership, and no local person with responsibility to maintain the church, it is perhaps not too surprising that, over time, people were tempted to "remove for safe keeping" items and artifacts from the church. Was there a more systematic plundering of the building, when the value of its contents, unguarded and apparently uncared for, was appreciated? Even the materials from which the building was constructed had a value to the 'right' people. Items such as the wonderful organ would have realized a good price as scrap.

Can it be classed as theft, if there is no owner to be found? This issue is a moral and legal maze and no doubt explains some people's reticence when the matter of the disappearing church is raised.

What makes the mystery even more astonishing is the presence of the burial ground next to the church, sadly now overgrown and vandalised with headstones and crosses broken off. Yet it is here that Gertrude Cass is buried and where Private D Crosby, a soldier of the First World War, brought to the Red Cross Hospital at the Manor House, was laid to rest, following a military funeral in the church on 1st December 1915.

The church and burial ground were actually conveyed by deed dated 7th July 1913 to the Rochester and Southwark Diocesan Church Trust. The Diocese would not agree to consecrate either church or burial ground if they did not own it. This was apparently a standard attitude. In fact, though, only the burial ground was ever consecrated, this being on 22nd May, 1913, a few weeks before the date of the deed. Lady Henry Somerset, Gertrude Cass, Lady Henry's sister Adeline, Duchess of Bedford and her son, Henry Charles Somers Somerset, were all party to this deed as Administrative Trustees.

By 1930, only Miss Cass and Somers Somerset of the original trustees, were still alive and it was belatedly realised that new trustees needed to be appointed, as there should be at least six. Miss Cass had the power to appoint new trustees and she named Lady Vernon, the Reverend Henry Ross of St Alban's Church in Holborn, Herbert Mason of East Sheen, Miss Selina Watson of Stow-on-the Wold, the Reverend Francis Baverstock of the Holy Family Homes, who was then living at Duxhurst, and Charles Radford Freeman, a solicitor, of Hanover Square, London.

Interestingly, there is a stipulation in the indenture of 1913 that the burial ground could be used as the burial ground for the following persons: Miss Gertrude Cass, Lady Henry Somerset and such other persons (including members of the colony and any other person associated with or interested in the work of the colony) as the Administrative Trustees agreed.

This is the only clue we have that, at this point in her life, Lady Henry was considering being buried herself at Duxhurst. It is a clear indication that she had, by this time, thrown off the shackles of her aristocratic background and had decided not to be buried in the family vault at Eastnor Castle. By the time of her death in 1921, she had apparently made other wishes known. Perhaps surprisingly, she had made it clear she wished to be buried out of her London church, St Alban's in Holborn, close to her flat in Gray's Inn and where her cousin the Reverend Russell officiated. As the cemetery for this church is part of the Victorian necropolis of Brookwood, near Woking, it is here that we find Lady

Henry's last resting place, a simple grave amongst hundreds of others. Perhaps this was the compromise for someone of her stature. We can not know whether the graveyard at Duxhurst would have been better maintained had Lady Henry been buried there, but the suspicion must be that it would have made little difference.

The graveyard today

Headstone of Gertrude Margaret Carew Cass.

The last burial appears to have been that of Miss Cass, who died on 14th March 1958. Her funeral service was held at Emmanuel Church, Sidlow with the Reverend A H Shergold officiating.

I have been unable to find any mention of the churchyard being officially closed for burials after this, but it seems Miss Cass's death marked the end of an era for the tiny graveyard.

As well as Miss Cass, her friend of many years Prisca Mary Graham, is buried here. Other graves mark the passing of Sister Linda (Alice Linda Cunningham) 1946, Sister Beatrice Payne (1930), Sister Lily (Mary Elizabeth Miller 1927) and Susan Edmonds "Laundry Matron and valued worker here" in 1930. Annie White, who died aged 61 on January 5th 1924, was probably also a worker on the estate.

Poignantly, there are several children's graves: Beatrice Joan Selvey, born August 4th 1903 "Entrusted to our care when she was a few weeks old", died 23rd October 1916; Jane Sybil Wigmore, died 24th May 1929 aged 4 years; Holland Archibald Holloway, died 1st June 1929 aged 3 years and Rosina Dwyer aged 16 whose simple wooden cross is so battered and neglected that its dates are illegible.

Father Robert S Lavies, who died on October 17th 1929 and who is remembered with such fondness by Violet Anthony, is also laid to rest here. His epitaph reads: "At the close of a faithful ministry He served as chaplain to this home Beloved by all its inmates."

There was also a provision in the 1913 document that if the Colony ceased to be carried on, or not to be used for a similar purpose which required use of a burial ground, then the Bishop of the Diocese could declare the burial ground to be held by the Rochester and Southwark

Diocesan Church Trust for the benefit of the inhabitants of the ecclesiastic parish in which Duxhurst was situated (now Sidlow parish).

There is another document dated 8th December 1930 which gives permission to The Holy Family Homes Incorporated (operating as The Lady Henry Somerset Homes at Duxhurst, Surrey) to use the church and burial ground subject to four undertakings: that the church be used for the performance of Divine Service according to the Liturgy and usages of the Church of England; that Holy Family Homes pay ten pounds per annum to the administrative trustees which would be used towards the cost of insurance of the building and then to maintain the burial ground in good order and repair; that Holy Family Homes maintained the church in good order and repair; that no structural alterations, internal or external, be made and no fixtures and fittings added or removed without the written consent of the administrative trustees.

Holy Family Homes Incorporated accepted these conditions in June 1931. There is an interesting additional clause:

"In giving this acceptance the Society recognises that the Administrative Trustees propose, as requested by the Imperial War Graves Commission … to give to that Commission an assurance that the grave of Private D. Crosby now in the Burial Ground shall remain permanently undisturbed."

According to the Commonwealth War Graves Commission, Private D Crosby's Duxhurst grave is not marked "as in or around 1966 the Commission erected a special memorial in Reigate (Redstone) Cemetery to commemorate him as the [Duxhurst] graveyard was even then in a state of neglect and the headstone could not be maintained." How sad!

Alongside this documentation is a Memorandum of Agreement, dated 20th October 1931, between Miss Cass and Holy Family Homes Incorporated which relates to the contents of the church, or chapel as it was called in the legal documentation, giving responsibility for the care and handling of the items to the Sister Superior of the Community of the Sacred Passion, at that time based in the Manor House at Duxhurst. The inventory takes up over six pages and provides a fascinating insight into how richly the church was furnished and equipped; from an old Italian walnut prayer table, ornate carved chairs, lamps, candlesticks, a 15th century Italian altar cloth, silver crucifix to the "organ as fitted in chamber and all its fitments and accessories." There were oil paintings and chalices designated as being of "special value", various chasubles (sleeveless vestments worn by the celebrant at Mass) including one "mounted with 14th century needlework embroidery", a Triple Sanctus bell and a small font, amongst the long list of items.

Many of these items would have been collected by Lady Henry on her travels abroad or sourced by Miss Cass.

The last service in the little church appears to have been on 12th September 1948, when Jennifer Mould was christened. Jennifer was the sister of Gina Knox (née Mould). The young family lived at that time in Somerset Cottage.

How sad it is that by the mid 1960s, the church was open to the elements, the lead having been stripped from the roof. The floor was littered with broken furniture and hymn books.

Former residents who had been at Duxhurst as children in the early 1900s were appalled at what was happening to their old homes. Violet Anthony (see Violet's story) and her friends Ethel and Winnie found it very distressing. In 1960 or 1961, Violet wrote to the Bishop of Guildford but got no response, so the three women enlisted their own children to help and loaded up a small van with several items including candlesticks, copper sconces, vestments and the calvary cross and took them to St Andrew's Church in Deal, with which Winnie and Ethel's family were still associated. They also rescued the Angelus bell. According to Ethel's son, Brian, "the chancel and calvary figures of the crucified Christ … together with the remains of a crucifix, were rotten from lying outside in the long grass, weeds and brambles and in need of much restoration." This restoration work was done by the Deal church and the calvary cross remounted. It remains at Deal today.

Figures from the Rood Screen now adorn a beautiful little church in West Sussex. These were given to St Michael and All Angels at Berwick by Alban Roe. His father, the Reverend Albert Roe was rector at Berwick from 1928 – 1934, after being Duxhurst's last chaplain from 1922 to 1928. The Bewick church is itself small but beautiful, and is now a Grade 1 listed building because of the murals painted during the Second World War by the famous Bloomsbury artists, Duncan Grant, Vanessa Bell and

Quentin Bell. The effect of the murals surrounding the rood screen is magnificent and this place seems a fitting home for the Duxhurst figures.

The Rood Screen at Berwick Church

There is a graphic description of the state of the Duxhurst church and the cottages in an article in *The News of the World* dated November 7th, 1965, written by Alan Whittaker:

"Perhaps the most startling relic of Duxhurst's past is the little church. Deadly nightshade grows around the porch. The heavy wooden door creaks eerily on rusty hinges. Hymn books and prayer books lie all over the floor, mildewed and yellow among the autumn leaves. Prayer cushions, gnawed by mice, rot in the gloom.

"Church furniture, broken and useless, has been scattered over the main hall. Fifty or so chairs are piled down one side. The raffia of the seats breaks at a touch.

"But the stained glass windows are intact. It is as though the vandals who have smashed every other window in the village had second thoughts.

"One window shows Raphael, the Angel of Healing. The window next to it is broken and a bramble has forced an entry."

Shortly after this article appeared, things got worse. Lead was stripped from the church roof and more and more of the contents mysteriously disappeared. The rural dean, the Reverend Neville Martin apparently tried to get the Diocese interested in the plight of the church and arranged for several of the more valuable items to be put into store with a local firm, Wakemans, but it seemed even here was not safe as the pieces then disappeared again.

A few items have resurfaced, safely kept in other churches. The font, for example, languished for several years in a barn on the Duxhurst farm and was at one time used as a bird bath, before being given to Emmanuel Church at Sidlow Bridge where it is still in use today.

Several chalices, alter cloths and copes are also kept at Emmanuel Church. Whilst the cloth may be disintegrating, the beauty of the articles is still apparent. Some items were subsequently fished out of the pond at Chipstead.

It must have been difficult for those who loved Duxhurst to stand idly by and watch the church fall into such disrepair. Tales of the Black Mass being celebrated in the church brought unwelcome newspaper interest to the village.

To prevent further vandalism and desecration of the church, it seems the central beam was pulled down, so the ceiling collapsed in on itself, effectively stopping anyone entering the building. The once delightful church of St Mary and the Angels was no more.

Font from St Mary and the Angels, now at Emmanuel Church, Sidlow

THE FINAL CURTAIN?

After the Second World War, when the military had all departed and the infants of the Alexandra Orphanage had moved to their new home at Gatton Park, squatters moved in to some of the vacant cottages at Duxhurst.

It was at this point that Miss Withers purchased the Duxhurst estate and began her long battle with the council to get permission for redevelopment. The low quality construction of the original cottages round the village green meant that they could not be patched up. A huge amount of money would have been required to bring them up to modern standards.

Yet people did live in them, some officially, others by stealth. Miss Withers would often rent cottages to her farm workers.

By the early fifties, one cottage, St Josephs, was rented by a Mrs Cresswell. She took in teenage boys as lodgers. It seems many of these were referred by the welfare officer of The Foundling Hospital. The philanthropic spirit of Duxhurst lived on.

One of the young men who stayed at Mrs Cresswell's was Gordon Aspey. By his own admission, Gordon was a difficult youngster. As he expresses it, he had not just a chip on his shoulder but a whole boulder. Having spent his early years at The Foundling Hospital and School, he was then reunited with his real mother and went to live with her, but this did not work out well. He fled back to London, desperately searching for lodgings and work. With no union ticket and few jobs available, he was destitute, so he made contact with one of the few people he knew who might help - Mr Kirk, the Welfare Officer of the Foundling Hospital. The kindly Mr Kirk told Gordon to catch a train to Reigate, where he would meet him at the station. He was taken straight to Mrs Cresswell's, joining five other young men there, whom Gordon recognized from his days at the Foundling School. The lads all had social problems; some had learning disabilities, but they all found a warm welcome at Duxhurst. Mr Kirk found Gordon a job at a coach builders in Redhill. Most of his meagre wages had to be paid over as rent to Mrs Cresswell, so he was always looking for extra jobs on the estate. He would work in Miss Withers' dairy in the evenings, eventually mastering the bottle washing machinery and at the weekends he would do the early morning deliveries. He remembers being given the task of cleaning out Miss Withers' green Citreon, which smelt foul from spilt milk. He also sprayed a car for one of the neighbours, managing to spray everything else in the vicinity as well!

Such was Gordon's nature at that time that he was frequently in trouble, especially over debts. He bought a bike but failed to keep up the instalments and couldn't resist a smart sports jacket to impress the local girls. He complained at work that the lunch Mrs Cresswell provided, four marmalade sandwiches and the occasional treat of stodgy bread pudding, was insufficient for a growing, working lad. Unbeknown to him, the works manager then contacted the Foundling Hospital. There was an ugly scene when Mr Kirk visited the Cresswell home to investigate the matter. Gordon was given his marching orders. Luckily for him, a neighbouring family, with whom he had become friendly, took him in so he remained at Duxhurst for a while longer.

Then he lost his job when redundancies were made by the coach firm. He worked on the farm and in the dairy, though he had disputes with Miss Withers about short payment and he accepts he did not take orders well. His dream was to buy his own motorbike. Almost inevitably, once he got one, he promptly fell off it and injured himself.

Gordon left Duxhurst when he was called up to do his National Service. He joined the RAF. From difficult beginnings, he has made a real success of his life. Undoubtedly, his short time at Duxhurst helped shape his character. His memoirs, *All at Sea*, make fascinating reading.

By the early 1960s Miss Withers was growing increasingly frustrated by the refusal of the Dorking and Horley Rural District Council to allow the village to be redeveloped. There were planning enquiries held, but no consent was forthcoming. The only use which would be considered for the centre of the village was 'institutional', as this would be an acceptable use within a green belt area.

In March 1962, a government inspector recommended that a purchase notice be confirmed whereby the Council bought the land from Miss Withers. Interestingly, this inspector seemed to have no knowledge of the origins of the Duxhurst village. He wrote, "The buildings when erected some 30 years ago were then flimsy and of sub-standard construction." He was wrong. The cottages were more than sixty years old at that point. Yet even if the heritage of the place had been understood, even if there had been some sympathy for the social history which permeated the cottages, the outcome of these planning enquiries would probably have been no different. The buildings were described as "very dilapidated and … well beyond that state when repair is a reasonable proposition from the owner's point of view."

Explaining that the Duxhurst estate fell within the proposed extension of the metropolitan green belt, the inspector decreed, "It is in the midst of a rural area and residential redevelopment on any scale would be sporadic, isolated and unjustifiable. There is no case for the perpetuation of the residential use of the land. Notwithstanding the present occupation of five of the cottages I find that the whole site can be held to have become incapable of reasonably beneficial use in its existing state."

As there was no sign of any buyer for institutional use, the council acquired the land. One of the uses they then considered was as a gypsy site, although it seems the gypsies themselves decided they preferred to go elsewhere, much to the relief of some of the locals.

In 1964, Surrey County Council approached the District Council about whether Duxhurst village might be a suitable location for an Approved School. The proposal was for "an Intermediate Approved School for boys accommodating an age range 13 to 16 years and would be for those needing special help with their education due to backwardness or sympathetic help in relation to personal problems." This scheme would certainly have continued the ethos of Duxhurst. The initial plans would have provided "a central block containing a hall, swimming bath and instructional rooms" as well as twelve houses or flats as staff accommodation. As extensive playing fields would also have been required, it was thought that some additional land might be purchased from Miss Withers in addition to that which had been compulsorily purchased in the village centre. Like many grand ideas before, these plans never came to fruition.

By now, Duxhurst village had a new neighbour a few miles to the south – Gatwick airport. The Managing Director of British United Airways Ltd thought Duxhurst would be an excellent location for his company's staff accommodation. "Almost anything" would improve the appearance of Duxhurst, he argued. "It was common knowledge that the premises were derelict and a haven for vermin and tramps." His staff urgently needed accommodation and there was a shortage of housing stock in the area. Duxhurst could provide the solution.

The council was unimpressed, although they seem to have kept a dialogue open with British United Airways Ltd for the next couple of years. At one point, a proposal to use part of the village as a training centre for staff was put forward as a possible way round the 'institutional use only' restriction on development.

Meanwhile the council was keen to find a vendor for the site, some person or organization who wished to acquire the land for a purpose acceptable within the green belt. Local agents were contacted. Informal approaches were made to charities such as The Abbeyfield Society. There was little interest. Whilst they dithered over the future of Duxhurst, the council did take one decisive action – they engaged The Reigate and District Rabbit Clearance Society to clear Duxhurst village of rabbits!

The council failed to appreciate that rabbits were the least of Duxhurst's problems. Abandoned properties had their attractions not just to rabbits, squirrels and rats but also to some of the local youths. Duxhurst became the 'in' place for parties and gatherings. The empty cottages provided shelter and seclusion – what did it matter if a careless match caused a little fire?

The estate attracted the attentions of the police following the Great Train Robbery in 1963. Ronald Biggs, one of the gang, lived in Redhill, so it was understandable that checks were made on all isolated communities and farms in the area, as the nationwide hunt for the criminals went on. However, there is no evidence that Duxhurst provided a refuge, even temporarily, for Biggs or any of his accomplices.

The Manor House found a new use, as a furniture repository for the Horley based store, W. H. Batchellor, now better known as Collingwood Batchellor. The firm had no use for the attractive grounds and gardens.

They became overgrown and neglected. Tony Morgan, who lived in Somerset Cottage, next door to the Manor House, in the late 1950s, described the grounds as being "like Sleeping Beauty's garden." The local fire brigade were apparently more worried about the furniture store going up in smoke than they were about the cottages, according to one ex-fireman. Once cleared of furniture, the building was boarded up – it, too, no longer met the needs of modern times.

The manor house prior to demolition. Photograph courtesy of Richard Cooper.

The very materials with which the cottages were so lovingly built in the 1890s now offered rich pickings. There appears to have been a slow, but systematic, plundering of the site. Even the chimneys disappeared; there one day, gone the next. The picturesque cottages, once a proud statement of hope and fresh beginnings, now crumbled, neglected and forlorn.

It was this sorry sight which greeted the reporter from the *News of the World* when he visited Duxhurst in November 1965. No wonder he declared the place "a ghost village. Decayed, deserted and almost forgotten."

The newspaper had probably been contacted by Mrs Allison, who was living in St Faiths, one of the cottages. She was a former actress, married to a Canadian army officer. The couple had three young children and an old Bentley, which undoubtedly looked somewhat incongruous parked outside their dilapidated home. Mrs Allison hoped press coverage of the family's poor living conditions might persuade the council to re-house the family elsewhere.

The journalist's description of the village is vivid: "Doors flap and creak painfully at the whim of the wind. Windows that were made for lace curtains and flower vases are now eyeless sockets, clearways for bats and owls. Floor boards and electric wiring have been ripped out."

The article refers to the origins of the village as "a village settlement for inebriated gentlewomen." Some of the working class women who lived in the cottages would no doubt have been amused to know they had been elevated to the ranks of 'gentlewomen', inebriated or not. The reporter also talks of Duxhurst being used during the Second World War, but there is no reference to its use in World War One. Memories had faded and his sources may not have known, or appreciated, the full history of the village.

As well as interviewing Mrs Allison, the journalist went into another of the cottages, St Josephs. "The fireplaces and the bath are still there although the place is falling apart. Floorboards are missing and broken glass litters the rooms." He tried to interview Miss Withers, who had little patience with his enquiries, trying to forbid him to visit the estate.

Two days after the article appeared, Dorking and Horley Rural District Council's Eastern Planning Committee took the decision to get a quotation for the demolition of the cottages. The Housing Officer reported that he had visited the site and found that "unauthorized use was being made of certain unoccupied, derelict buildings." This was very probably the same Housing Officer who had refused to see or talk to the *News of the World* reporter when he had been making enquiries prior to publication. Clearly, the bad publicity was having some effect.

Of course, the wheels of bureaucracy turn very slowly and in the interim the newspaper article only served to attract more undesirable elements to the area. The vandalism continued unabated. Potential offers for the land to be used as a pig farm, or for storage of building materials, were refused by the Council.

One has to feel sympathy for the occupiers of the few remaining substantial properties along Duxhurst Lane. By September 1967, Mr Hallas, who lived in Meadowlands, wrote to the council on behalf of some of the locals. He expressed their concerns about the state of the derelict buildings. They were aware that the council had obtained one quote, of £675, for the demolition of the buildings. The local residents thought this was very high and were suggesting that the council passed the responsibility for demolition to them. They would organize the work and the removal of the rubble for just £350. If it cost them more, they would bear the extra cost themselves.

The Eastern Planning Committee decided the matter was now beyond their terms of reference and passed the issue over to the council's General Purposes Committee. They asked Mr Hallas to obtain an estimate for the work. One was quickly provided, from Hilden Demolition, for £400 for the demolition of eight cottages and outhouses. This prompted the Housing Officer to seek other quotations. The council clearly did not want local residents taking charge of the operation.

On the 30th October 1967, Dorking and Horley Rural District Council's General Purposes Committee accepted a quote from P.G. Stapleton, which they had negotiated down to a figure of £275 – a small price to pay to wipe out such a fascinating piece of social history! But the buildings were "dangerous and attracting undesirable persons." Action was at last planned. There was just one problem – the Allison family still lived in one of the cottages. Interestingly council minutes refer to Mr and Mrs Allison as "acting as resident caretakers", a fact not widely recognized by others in the area. The Eastern Housing Committee were asked to re-house the Allisons in suitable accommodation, as and when it became available.

However, tragedy almost occurred before the family moved out, for the following spring their cottage caught fire. Gina Knox remembers the young boy, Robin Allison, dashing down the lane towards her, calling for help. Thankfully, the fire brigade arrived in time to prevent total collapse and no-one was injured. The incident spelled the end for the cottages. There was another fire, perhaps caused by youths enjoying a party amongst the ruins, then the bulldozers moved in. Tons of spoil were dumped on the site. The centre of Duxhurst was not only dead; it had been buried.

Yet there were a few buildings remaining along Duxhurst Lane. What was their future to be?

CUSTODIANS OF A SPECIAL HERITAGE

Following local government restructuring and boundary changes in 1974, Duxhurst became part of the Borough of Reigate and Banstead. Miss Withers took the opportunity to buy back the land which had been compulsorily purchased from her and she continued to farm many acres, employing a succession of farm managers. Some barns and sheds were abandoned to their fates. The remains of a large milking shed can still be seen. One of the Dutch barns was sold and moved to nearby Norwood Hill where it is still used today.

Duxhurst farmhouse fell into disrepair. Although some people were keen to buy it after Miss Withers' death, it was let by her family to the council. Some youngsters were housed there for a while but they seemed to lack the support they needed. Their behaviour caused problems and they were eventually evicted. The property was left vandalised and fire-damaged. It lay dilapidated for many years, but in 2006 permission was granted, on appeal, for it to be demolished so that a new house could be built on the site.

Perhaps surprisingly, given the council's refusal to countenance any redevelopment of the central cottages, permission was granted in 1960 to replace the small bungalow along the lane. Local builder, Mr Gatwood, built the new property. William (Willie) Constable, who lived at Lower Duxhurst Farm, just opposite the entrance to Duxhurst, suggested that his parents bought this bungalow for their retirement home. The Constables had done various work for Miss Withers over the years and Willie still does odd jobs for Duxhurst residents, with his tractor and hedge cutting equipment. He has a great feel for the heritage of the village and tried for many years to keep the churchyard under control, fighting a losing battle with both vandals and nature. The present owners of the bungalow have recently secured planning permission to extend their home, in keeping with its 1960s style.

Gina and Peter Knox remained at Somerset Cottage until 1998. For twenty years, Gina had continued the 'education' theme of Duxhurst life, not only raising her own family but running a playgroup at her home. Duxhurst again provided a wonderful playground for children.

Arthur Hutchinson, an architect for the Department of the Environment, lived for many years at St Mary's (now Duxhurst Place). Arthur was a keen local historian and a skilled artist. He drew a pictorial map of Duxhurst, copies of which still exist today. In the 1980s, Arthur, together with John Norsworthy and Audrey Ward, used to give talks locally about the history of Duxhurst, ensuring its story was known to a new generation. John, former headmaster of High Trees School, who attended the school himself during its Duxhurst years, wrote a booklet *Beauty to Ashes* (the title a tribute to Lady Henry Somerset's own book *Beauty for Ashes*) but this was never widely published.

The rear of Duxhurst Place today looks remarkably similar to how it appeared, as St Mary's, in the 1936 auction particulars.

The manor house was eventually demolished but many of the bricks were painstakingly cleaned up and reused to build a new house, Sidlow Manor. The Searle family did all the hard work, living in a caravan on site, but then sold the house to realize their profit rather than move in themselves.

This property takes up about three quarters of the footprint of the original manor. There are still some remnants of the original building linked in with the new design.

There are exposed foundations of other buildings, probably the army huts erected during the First World War when the house was used as a Red Cross Hospital. One undated plan, probably from the 1930s, shows a boot repair depot here.

Rear of Duxhurst Place (formerly St Mary's). Photograph taken courtesy of the current owner.

Sidlow Manor (The Manor House). Photographs taken by kind permission of the current owner.

The Cottage in 1962. Photographs courtesy of Peter Green

The Cottage with tiled roof in the 1970s

The Cottage, the original home of Lady Henry Somerset and then Gertrude Cass, was bought in 1962 from Miss Withers by the Greens, whose son, Peter, still lives there today. It was in a poor state of repair, with most of the thatch on the ground in the courtyard. The new family could only gain access by climbing in through the windows!

It is interesting to see how the house looked when a new tiled roof was put on it in the 1970s.

The property was subsequently re-thatched.

Peter takes great pride in the history of his house. With his permission, I have been able to take photographs of the property in 2011, to mirror those which appeared in The Ideal Home Magazine in 1923, as can be seen on the following pages. Many of the original features remain, including the cylindrical chimney and the oval window.

Following the death of Miss Withers, much of the estate was eventually bought up by Rotch Property Company, owned by the Iranian Tchenguiz brothers. Outline planning permission was granted for a golf course, with an agreed change of use from agricultural land. Reserved matters were approved in 1993, but the permission was allowed to lapse.

Then, in 2002, an ambitious plan for two eighteen-hole golf courses, plus a golf academy and club house, was submitted to the council. The proposals required the demolition and conversion of several buildings and the importation of fill material, to create the necessary contours for the golf courses. By 2004, this scheme had been withdrawn, only for new plans to be submitted in January 2006. This time there was to be just one eighteen-hole course, with a practice ground and associated club house, maintenance building and car park. The imported fill would be significantly reduced, but the council still had issues about this.

In December 2009, the planning application was finally refused, one of the grounds being concerns over financial viability. There was a perceived risk that if the project was started but left unfinished, the land could not easily, or cheaply, be restored to its former state. In the light of recent events, with the economic downturn, the collapse of the property boom and the subsequent investigation into Robert and Victor Tchenguiz's business affairs, this may have been a wise decision.

Certain parcels of land, particularly on the left hand side of Duxhurst

Lane coming from the A217, have now been bought by owners of neighbouring properties. Improvements have been made to verges and pathways. The main estate has been sold to an Irish agricultural company, so farming should continue at Duxhurst.

The heart of the village may have long gone, but the residents of the few remaining properties enjoy their rural idyll. Rabbits, pheasants, guinea fowl and deer make homes there. The threat of development has retreated and it is time once more to appreciate the heritage of Duxhurst. That final curtain hasn't quite fallen.

The porch of the cottage, showing the della Robbia angel over the entrance. Showing, also, the extension of the cottage. This was added by Lady Somers, in order to provide an upstairs bedroom.

E 375

From The Ideal Home Magazine 1923

The same room today

From The Ideal Home Magazine 1923

The cylindrical chimney is still in place today

EPILOGUE

2011 brings the story of Duxhurst to a close on an uplifting note. Emmanuel Church at Sidlow, in whose parish Duxhurst sits, is this year celebrating its one hundred and fiftieth anniversary. The history of the parish is being promoted.

Members of the church are working with the Diocese to see if some responsibility for the upkeep of the Duxhurst graveyard can be established. It would be wonderful to think that the last resting place of Miss Cass, and some of the other characters in the drama of Duxhurst, might be rescued from the brambles.

On June 19th 2011, an open air service will be held at Duxhurst. The air will once again be filled with voices raised in praise of God. The final curtain is being raised for an encore. Lady Henry Somerset would approve.

Bibliography

Works by Lady Henry Somerset:

Our Village Life (1884)

Beauty for Ashes (L. Upcott Gill & Sons, Ltd 1913)

Other books:

Lady Henry Somerset by Kathleen Fitzpatrick (Jonathan Cape 1923)

Discovering Reigate Priory – the Places and the People by Audrey Ward (Bluestream Books 1998)

Aristocracy, Temperance and Social Reform –the life of Lady Henry Somerset by Olwen Claire Niessen (Tauris Academic Studies 2007)

Writing Out My Heart - Selections from the Journal of Frances E. Willard edited by Carolyn De Swarte Gifford (University of Illinois 1995)

Noble Work by Noble Women by Jennie Chappell (S. W. Partridge & Co., London 1900)

The Victorians by A.N. Wilson (Random House Group Limited 2005)

Victorian People by Gillian Avery (Collins 1970)

Beauty to Ashes by John Norsworthy (unpublished)

A Century of Service 1876 – 1976 (The National British Women's Total Abstinence Union Centenary booklet)

A History of Reigate Priory by Ernest Scears

High Trees School – The History of a School near Horley by Brian Buss & Richard Cooper

All at Sea – Memories of a Coram Boy by Gordon Aspey (Emsea Press 2010)

Villages of Character by Hutch (Arthur Hutchinson) (1986)

Nightingale of the North by Amy Peyton (1983)

*From Rags to Riches –*Lilian Brown's memories (unpublished)

Social Scenes of Yesterday - Glimpses of Reigate and Redhill 1900-1920 by Alan Ingram

Sources

At the heart of the story of Duxhurst are the personal stories I have been told. I have tried to support and confirm these, wherever possible, by reference to other sources, including documents and articles at:

Eastnor Castle archives

British Women's Temperance Association archives

The Times archives

The British Library and the National Newspaper archives at Colindale

Surrey History Centre

Unfortunately I have been unable to discover any of the patient records for Duxhurst and suspect these may have been destroyed.

Historians who desire more detailed information on the source of any material within the book are welcome to contact me by email: lhs.ros@googlemail.com

Index